A SEASON OF CHANGE

A SEASON OF CHANGE

GWENDOLYN HARMON

Learning Ladyhood Press

To Aunt Carol, with love.

Contents

I

Morning at Miss Harriet's

Katherine woke in the grey light of dawn, jolted out of sleep by her alarm. Switching on the light, she squeezed her brown eyes shut against the sudden brightness. As she waited for the pain to subside and her eyes to adjust to the light, she stretched a little and sighed. Never in her life had she been so bone-weary tired as she felt this morning.

Easing her eyes open, she gazed around the room. How long ago it seemed now since she first came to Miss Harriet's tea shop, looking for a fresh start. Little had she known then how much she would come to love the prim little shop and its gentle owner, who had become her dearest friend.

Katherine's eyes drooped, but she forced herself to turn and look at the clock. There was no time to drift off, not even for a few minutes. She needed to get the baking in.

Swinging her feet to the floor, she reluctantly stood, feeling every muscle. She had never imagined running a tea shop could make a person so sore.—Or maybe it was the boxes she had ferried to the Harborside's storeroom last evening.

Captain Braddock did offer to make do without her while Miss Harriet was away, but Katherine had insisted. She closed Miss Harriet's an hour early each day so she could at least get a little of her regular work done at the Harborside. Time spent at the old tea seller's historic shop always relaxed her, somehow.

Katherine pulled some clothes out of the closet and dragged herself through the process of getting ready for the day.

Why is this so hard? It wasn't as if this were the first time she had run the shop alone. But then again, Miss Harriet's Tearoom was far less busy in those days. Things had really picked up since they joined forces with the Harborside to pair people with their perfect cup of tea. In fact, business had boomed for both shops.

As she brushed her teeth, Katherine mentally calculated how many more early mornings were left before Miss Harriet would return. She and the town's reporter, Harold James, had been away on their honeymoon for four days now, which meant Katherine had only three more days left of baking, waiting tables, and washing dishes alone.

Captain Braddock missed her help at the Harborside, but did his best to take up the slack. And she still stopped by after closing to help with restocking.

Running a brush through her wavy brown curls, she quickly pulled her hair up into a bun. The few hours at the

Harborside were a welcome change of pace, even though it meant one more responsibility to add to her already full days.

Katherine suddenly wondered what she would do if ever Captain Braddock went away and left her to handle the Harborside. But no, that wasn't very likely.

The last in a long succession of Braddocks, the aging captain seemed as rooted in Harborhaven as his shop, which had stood on Main Street longer than most of the town had even existed. She supposed the only thing that might tempt him away would be a visit to his sister Serena in China, but though he was a retired sea captain, Katherine couldn't quite picture him as a world traveler.

No, he wasn't likely to leave, and that was a good thing, because the very thought of it made Katherine feel even more weary.

Crossing to the window seat in the small apartment's living room, she switched on a lamp and pulled a blanket from the basket nearby. Curling up with the blanket, she picked up her Bible.

Ok, Lord, she prayed, *I know I can't do this without Your help. I'm so tired. Please refresh me.* Then, she opened her Bible to where she had left off the day before and began reading.

* * * *

The soft glow of the golden September sunshine had just begun to filter through the lace curtains of Miss Harriet's tea shop as Katherine descended the stairs from her apartment above. Her muscles still ached, but her heart and mind felt renewed.

Stopping halfway, she took a deep breath and surveyed the peaceful scene. Rows of small tables dotted the cleanly polished wood floors, each covered with a dainty lace tablecloth and a vase of flowers. The straight-backed wood chairs stood ready to receive the day's first customers, and the chalkboard menu had been freshly written the night before.

How glad Katherine was that Miss Harriet had trained her to make everything as ready as possible for the next day before leaving for the night! It made such an encouraging start to the morning's work to know that there was nothing left from yesterday.

She pulled aside the curtain which served as the kitchen door and stepped into the now-familiar routine of early morning baking. As she pulled out bowls and canisters and began measuring ingredients, she thought of the first batch of scones she had tried to bake and had to chuckle. They had been terribly rubbery and greasy, but Miss Harriet was a patient teacher, and insisted she try again.

Now she almost mindlessly flew through the recipes which had seemed so daunting to her when she first began helping with the baking. This morning was no exception, and the first batches of scones and pastries were soon ready for the oven.

Katherine was just setting the big kettle on to boil when she was summoned out of the kitchen by a rap on the door. As she pulled aside the lace curtain, she felt her heart lift in astonished surprise at the sight of Captain Braddock!

The elderly sea captain's short grey hair peeked out from under the captain's hat he always wore, though he had retired years ago. He smiled at Katherine as she unlocked the door, blue eyes twinkling, the scar across his cheek melting into the waves of wrinkles that crinkled up his weatherbeaten face.

"Good mornin' Missy. I've brought yer tea order early, so you don't have to worry about sellin' out before the end of the day."

Her heart lifted at the thoughtfulness of this gruff old man who had become just like family to her. "Thank you. It will be nice to know we won't run out of anything today. Won't you come in for a cup of tea before opening time?"

Captain Braddock looked over her shoulder at the flowers and frills of the dainty room and frowned doubtfully. "Yer sure it's not heapin' extra work on you?"

"I'm sure. And besides, the company will be nice while I get the trays prepped."

"Well, I suppose it won't hurt to come in, just for a little."

Katherine smiled. It had taken a long time for Captain Braddock to get to the point of stepping foot into Miss Harriet's, and he still never seemed quite comfortable when he did. The two tea-sellers had been somewhat at odds when Katherine first arrived in Harborhaven.

A misunderstanding and a lost letter sparked it all off, and differences of opinion over types and qualities of tea exacerbated what residents of Harborhaven quickly came to view as a feud between the two shops. But now, all was resolved and the two had become unlikely friends—although Captain Braddock still looked askance at the teabags she kept in stock alongside the higher quality loose-leaf tea.

"If you sit here, we can talk while I get the tea ready." Katherine said, showing the captain to a table right by the kitchen doorway.

"All right." The captain groaned slightly as he eased himself into the dainty dining chair facing the kitchen door. "What do you want to talk about?"

Katherine grinned and called over her shoulder, "Whatever company talks about, I suppose."

"Well, now...I don't much know what company talks about. When I was a boy, everyone talked about the weather when they went visiting. That, or politics."

"Oh. Weather then, please."

The captain chuckled. "It's been mighty fine of late. I don't think we'll be firing up the old stove for a good while yet."

"That's good. I don't think I've quite gotten the hang of it yet. I'm always nervous I'll let the shop get too hot and ruin all the tea, or that the fire will die out as soon as I turn my back."

"I used to feel the same way about it, but I suppose it's grown on me. Or perhaps it's necessity that's driven me to appreciate it. Whatever the case, I must say it's nice during these warm days to have one less thing to keep track of, 'specially right now."

Katherine came out of the kitchen and dropped wearily into a chair across from the captain. "I know. Things will be back to normal soon, though. Only a few more days."

"Three, to be exact."

Katherine chuckled. "I thought I was the only one counting the days!"

Captain Braddock's smile softened. "I can see how hard it is on you, keepin' everything goin' on your own. And as much as I hate to see you worn down, I'm proud of you for steppin' up and not makin' excuses."

A warm glow spread over Katherine's heart. Captain Braddock rarely voiced his feelings, and somehow, a word of encouragement from his grandfatherly heart felt like being handed a priceless treasure. Unsure what to say in reply, Katherine just smiled happily across the table, and Captain Braddock smiled right back at her.

The singing of the tea kettle interrupted the brief silence.

"I'd better get that." Katherine said, rising from her chair and hurrying toward the kitchen.

"Sure I can't help with anything?" Captain Braddock called after her.

"Not a thing. Just you sitting there is a help." She poked her head around the doorway with a teasing grin. "And if you're good, I'll bring some scones in with the tea. They'll be ready to come out of the oven soon."

"Then I'll be stayin' put, for sure," he replied with a wink. "What kind of scones are they?" he called out as Katherine disappeared into the kitchen again.

"Cheddar," Katherine called back, swirling hot water around the teapot to warm it, just like Captain Braddock had taught her to do. "They're Mr. James' favorite, and he's always been our first customer of the day, so they've always been baked first. Then, we put in Mrs. Penelope's fluffy round scones, although she has been branching out a bit now that she eats with Mr. Patten every day."

"Think the two of them'll ever follow in yer employer's footsteps?"

"Possibly. I hope so, anyway. They're such a sweet couple, and both being older, I think it's just so wonderful for them to have each other."

Captain Braddock eyed her closely as she brought the tea tray to the table. "Yer not feelin' left out, now are you?"

"No," Katherine replied, taking her seat across from the captain. "Not yet, anyway. I'm sure I will eventually, but for the moment, I'm just happy for Miss Harriet. Besides, I haven't had any time to feel left out yet." She lifted the dainty Royal Albert teapot and poured a dark liquid into the matching cups.

"This the new blend?" Captain Braddock asked, as Katherine handed him his cup and saucer.

"Yes. I thought you might like to try it out with me."

"I can taste the Assam..." He took another sip. "And there's the Ceylon. I wouldn't have thought to blend the two, but this is quite good."

"Good thing you listened to me, then," Katherine said with a teasing grin. She tasted her own tea. "You're right. It is good." Holding out a plate, she added, "Scone?"

Captain Braddock picked a golden-brown triangle and plunked it down on his plate, saying thoughtfully, "You know, the newlyweds have presented the town with quite a dilemma."

"How so?"

"Well, here we all are, used to saying 'Miss Harriet', and she's gone and become 'Mrs. James.' Even you aren't calling her by her proper name yet."

"That's true. I know she isn't thinking of changing the shop's name, but the rest of us do need to figure out what to call her."

"How do the customers handle it?"

"Oh, they mostly still call her 'Miss Harriet.' Rosie calls her

'*Miz* Harriet'—when she remembers to." Katherine shook her head over this latest piece of presumption by their gossipy regular with a penchant for tabloids and flamboyant hats.

Captain Braddock chuckled. "That doesn't seem to fit at all."

"I agree. It would be easier if everyone called her just 'Harriet,' but people can't seem to do it. Even I don't call her that. So, Mrs. James it must be, I suppose. But it's going to be a difficult habit to change."

"Sure will. There may be lots of changes in the next little while. You just keep yer feet settled on yer own path, and don't get too attached to life as it has been."

Katherine frowned and cupped her tea in her hands to warm them. "What do you mean?"

"Only that things are bound to be different in lots of ways, now that Miss Harriet—Mrs. James, that is, has a husband to go home to at the end of the day."

"I suppose we probably won't be able to linger over the washing up like we used to..." Katherine's voice trailed off. The nightly ritual of dishwashing had been a highlight of Katherine's time at Miss Harriet's. The two would discuss just about everything; the day, the customers, the books they were reading. It was a relaxing end to a busy day, and Katherine knew it just wouldn't be the same without her dear friend to talk to.

Captain Braddock's brows furrowed as he watched the change in her expression. "Now, here I am pourin' doom and gloom on yer day, and yer mornin's barely begun! Fine company I am!" He reached across the table and patted her hand.

"Don't you worry, Missy. You'll be just fine, so long as you keep yer focus right."

Katherine gave his hand a gentle squeeze. "I know." She sighed. There's just so much going on right now—" A genteel chime sounded from behind the curtained doorway, and Kathrine grinned. "Such as the morning baking. I'll just get that next batch into the oven."

She hurried into the kitchen with a full heart and busy mind, determined to follow the captain's advice and stay focused on the tasks at hand, not wanting to think about how things might be about to change.

2

A Family Business

The sun had already begun its descent into the blue-grey of the harbor as Katherine locked the door of Miss Harriet's and started out across Harborhaven's historic downtown blocks. Here and there the sinking sun squeezed its way between the tall masses of elaborate Victorian brick, bathing everything it touched in a vibrant shade of gold.

Katherine stooped and picked up a bright leaf from among many on the sidewalk. The weather may have been mild so far, but the trees certainly knew what season it was.

Autumn always seemed to sneak up on Katherine now. Perhaps it was because she was too busy, too distracted to watch for it. As a child, she would notice each leaf, each change in the temperature from one day to the next, savoring the coming of fall as it unfurled bit by bit before her eyes.

But now—she sighed and twirled the leaf between her fingers. These days, it seemed like the change was nearly over before she even noticed it had begun. Perhaps someday she would have time to savor the seasons again.

Loosening her fingers to let the breeze carry her leaf away, she strode onwards. There was much to do at the Harborside tonight. And then it would be back to Miss Harriet's to finish the washing up and polish the counter before going to bed. She took a deep breath. *Three more days.*

* * * *

"Hello there, Katherine. Profitable day?" Captain Braddock met Katherine at the door and helped her off with her jacket.

"Almost too profitable. The lunch rush had people waiting on the sidewalk, there were so many at once. Here's our restock order." Katherine fished a piece of paper from her pocket and handed it to the captain.

"I brought you more of the Don Chong Oolong this morning."

"I know... it's the Luncheon Society. Rosie's forbidden them from asking for a recommendation. Instead, she has the whole tableful of them ordering the same tea, and she's working her way down the tea list one week at a time." Katherine pulled the stiff navy apron off its hook by the door and slipped it wearily over her head, then glanced back at Captain Braddock with a weak smile. "She's calling it, 'the grand tour' and insisting we should feature it on the menu—and name it after her, of course."

"I'm sure she is." Captain Braddock chuckled a little, but as Katherine peeked at the large jars under the counter to see which needed to be refilled, she glanced up and saw his bushy white eyebrows scrunch together into a look of concern. "That employer of yers oughtta hire someone on to help you when she goes off gallivantin' like this."

"It isn't frivolous gallivanting, she's on her honeymoon. Besides, we talked about it before the trip, but neither of us could think of anyone suitable." She shrugged and walked into the back office, the little room she had nicknamed the "Captain's Quarters." Reaching up, she took a clipboard from the wall.

"Still. I can't help thinkin' it's too much on you all at once."

Katherine shrugged again, then glanced up from the clipboard with a little smirk. "You know, Miss Harriet isn't my *only* employer."

Captain Braddock folded his arms and stood tall. "You might have noticed, Missy, just what *kind* of business we have here?"

"Um... a tea business?" Katherine replied slowly, uncertain where the captain was headed.

"Yes, but this also happens to be a *family* business. Right from the beginning, when Captain Jeremiah Braddock unloaded his first cargo of tea right into this very room, the Harborside has been a family business. Every generation of Braddocks has grown up, right here, working alongside the rest of the family." Captain Braddock fell silent, gazing into the storefront.

Katherine knew that look—the look of memories flooding in, and the inevitable wave of sadness close behind. She thought it must be so hard to be the last generation, with only one sister left —and her in a distant land—out of what had been a close-knit bundle of aunts, uncles, grandparents, and great-grandparents all living, working, laughing, and crying together.

With just a hint of emotion in his voice, he turned back to Katherine and fixed her in one of his serious frowns. "We don't have *employees* here, Katherine. Never did, never will. We only have *family*. And don't you forget it." With that, he turned and went back into the shop, his characteristic limp making an uneven staccato of footsteps on the time-worn wood of the floorboards.

Katherine stared after him, eyes blurred with tears. She knew Captain Braddock thought of her as belonging to the Harborside, and Katherine herself thought of it as home, but he had never used that momentous word before.

Yes, family was the thing most precious to Captain Braddock's heart—so much so that he had nearly sacrificed his entire retirement savings in order to keep the Harborside running and his family's legacy alive.

Family. She felt the word sink warmly into the deepest part of her heart. She wished she could go in and tell the captain just how much that word meant to her, but she knew Captain Braddock too well. He had made a gesture, shown his heart, and now it was done. He would want everything to just go on as it was before.

No fuss, that was the captain. He would drop his reserve momentarily, then the wall would go right back up again, even higher and thicker than before. Katherine always wondered why he did that, but she knew better than to try to push her way past the wall. She would find some way to show

him how she valued the honor of being Harborside family...
but what?

With full heart and mind, she turned her attention to
the task at hand. Inventory in the chilly storage room didn't
appeal to Katherine's aching muscles, but it had to be done.
Opening the heavy wood door, she flipped on the light and
got to work.

3

Mrs. James

Katherine had just put in the morning baking when she heard the rattle of a key in the lock, followed by the cheery jingle of the bell over the door.

"Hello, Dearie!"

A burst of joy thrilled through Katherine as she heard the familiar voice. Rushing out from the kitchen, she found herself wrapped in a motherly embrace. "Miss Harriet! I didn't expect you this early. Why, you haven't even been home yet, have you?"

"No. I wanted to surprise you and make sure you were still alive after bearing the full burden of the shop for an entire week!"

"Only just. It's so much busier now than when you went away before!" Stepping back, Katherine surveyed her friend. Tall, elegant, with her glossy blonde hair twisted up into a flawless French roll, she looked every inch the gracious

English lady Katherine knew her to be. Her usual floral skirt and pastel cardigan gave her a put-together look that seemed to seep out from her very core. Her face usually wore a look of sweet and happy serenity, but this morning, she looked as though she might burst with joy. "You look perfectly radiant."

"Thank you. I must say, married life suits me so far."

"I suppose that's a good thing," quipped Katherine with a wink.

The shop bell rang again and Harold James stepped in, arrayed in his usual attire of tweed jacket, white collared shirt, dark slacks, and well-shined leather shoes. He held a tweed cap in one hand and reached out to shake Katherine's hand with the other.

"Hello, Katherine. How has it gone for you?"

"Pretty well. I must admit, I've never been happier to see Miss—that is... Mrs..." Katherine turned toward her friend. "Actually, I've been wondering, what exactly *do* we call you now?"

With a blush, the new bride looked adoringly at her husband and said sweetly, "Well, Dearie, I'm rather partial to *Mrs. James.*"

"What a coincidence—so am I!" the tall reporter interjected with a wink, putting an arm around his new bride.

"Mrs. James it is, then... but it will take a while to get used to saying it." Katherine smiled. The two were obviously still basking in the glow of newlywedded life. She couldn't be happier for them, but now that they were standing right there in front of her in all their happiness, Katherine felt an odd little tug, somewhere off in a far corner of her heart, a nagging thing she couldn't quite shake.

"Well, Dearie, here we are, barging in on you first thing, with no respect at all for your morning baking! Can I help you with anything?"

"I just got the first batch of scones in, and the rest are all ready to go. Why don't you two sit at your usual table and I'll make you some tea?—Unless you need to get home. I'm sure you're tired after all that travelling."

"I am, a bit... but you know there's nothing like a good cup of tea for setting me right again." She looked up at her new husband. "What do you say, Darling?"

"Harriet, I'd give you the moon if you asked it." he pulled a serious face, but his dark brown eyes flashed out a twinkle as he added, "However, as you're far too sensible to ask for that, I'll gladly spring for a cup of tea in lieu of the moon."

"Right. I'll set the water on to boil." Katherine was almost to the kitchen when Mr. James called out,

"And, Katherine?"

She stopped and turned towards him. "Yes?"

"Any chance of a cheddar scone?"

She grinned. "Fresh from the oven any minute now."

"Wonderful! It's good to be *home* again!"

* * * *

The day flew by, just as busy as the day before, yet just knowing Miss Harriet was home buoyed Katherine's spirits. How she would ever get used to calling her "Mrs. James," Katherine didn't know, but she wanted to honor her friend's joy in her new title. The couple lingered over their breakfast long enough to greet many of the "dailies," those faithful customers who came in every day.

The sight of the new Mr. and Mrs. James in the tea shop seemed to put everyone in a good mood, although Rosie did grab Katherine's sleeve as she passed and confide in a stage whisper, "They seem so happy... I only hope it lasts. Most don't, you know. I was just reading the other day..." She then launched into a lurid account she had probably read in one of the tabloids she habitually carried around in her purse. When Katherine finally got away, she wondered if Rosie would ever find something uplifting to talk about.

The elderly widow everyone called Mrs. Penelope used to be one of their very first customers of the day, but now came in later to eat with Mr. Patten, the town's senior—and only— bank officer. The genteel pair arrived at the tea shop in the eleven o'clock quiet before the lunch rush—the "calm before the storm," as Miss Harriet called it. They shared a pot of Earl Grey, two Cornish pasties, and a plate of the small, round, fluffy scones Mrs. Penelope used to order each morning. They would talk quietly while they ate, and when they finished, Mr. Patten would offer his arm and the two would stroll out the door and down the street.

Then the lunch rush would hit, beginning with the inevitably dramatic arrival of Rosie a little while before noon. She would burst through the door, causing the bell overhead to jangle in a peculiarly boisterous way, and would plunk herself down in a seat near the front window, breathless—but never speechless—with the excitement of whatever "news" she had to tell.

Sometimes it was an account of a local drama, such as

the time a tree fell in the parking lot of the local elementary school. Rosie's theory was that some of the kids were trying to get out of a test, and figured if the parking lot got blocked, they would have the day off. Official reports on the tree came back with a verdict of "natural causes," although no one had been able to convince Rosie it wasn't some kind of a plot.

Rosie's visits never lasted less than an hour, and usually involved craning her head to see as far down Main Street as possible, in order to keep tabs on what everyone in Harborhaven was up to. Often, she would be joined by six or seven similarly gossipy ladies—all in outlandish hats—who called themselves "the Luncheon Club." How this club got started, Katherine didn't know, but they seemed to have been coming to Miss Harriet's just about as long as the shop had been open.

Rosie was their chosen leader, although Katherine wondered if the group really had much choice about the matter. But they were loyal to a fault, and whatever Rosie said, the ladies of the Luncheon Club heartily echoed, whether it was true or false.

The lunch rush was an odd jumble of tourists and locals that day, and Katherine felt nearly run off her feet trying to keep everyone's orders straight and deliver them to the right tables in a timely manner. Most of the tourists came looking to be matched up with their "perfect" cup of tea, a skill Katherine had learned from Captain Braddock during her first year at the Harborside. That was what caused the uptick in business for both the shops, since Miss Harriet's began to stock a wider variety of tea in order to provide what each different customer would like.

Harborhaven had been famous once, long ago, as the home of the Harborside tea sellers, where the Braddock family would tell people *exactly* which kind of tea would suit them best. This ability, which seemed to outsiders like some kind of magic, really just came down to careful observation. But Katherine was pleased to have picked up "the Braddock gift," as it was called. It gave her a feeling of being somehow connected to the Harborside, to its history, and to the history of Harborhaven.

Katherine wheeled the little tea cart out from the kitchen and began collecting the last round of teacups, saucers, plates, and silverware from the lace covered tablecloths. Hearing the bell over the door, she turned to see Miss Harriet headed for the kitchen, rolling up her sleeves as she walked. Returning with a fluttery apron tied over her floral skirt and pastel blouse and cardigan, she quietly began clearing the dishes from a table near where Katherine was working.

"It's good to have you here." Katherine said, adding a saucer to the stack on the cart.

"It's good to be back." The new Mrs. James said with a smile. "Do you know, I actually missed washing up at the end of the day?"

Katherine grinned. "Well, you're welcome to it any time!"

The two moved the cart to the next set of tables and got to work. Pausing by the cart, Mrs. James surveyed Katherine with a thoughtful look.

"You look entirely done in, Katherine. Tell me how things really went while I was away?"

Katherine took a deep breath. There would be no glossing over things with this tall, graceful, motherly woman.

Wrestling with her pride, Katherine finally responded. "It was rough. The lunch rush alone was exhausting and, combined with the baking and my usual jobs of waiting tables. tracking and ordering inventory of the different teas, it was a lot. I don't know how you did it alone all those years."

"The shop was less busy then, and we offered far less selection. Mind you, the tourists are good for business. I knew it would be difficult, and I hated leaving you to handle it all by yourself. This just isn't a one-man operation anymore." The two fell into silence as they finished clearing the last few tables and wheeled the cart into the kitchen.

Katherine turned the water on and squirted the dish soap into the sink for the delicate China cups and saucers. She stared pensively at the bubbles. There was something on her employer's mind, something she was waiting for the right moment to share. The nagging something in a back corner of Katherine's heart suddenly flooded over her and a knot began to tighten in the pit of her stomach. Suddenly, she was afraid of the conversation about to unfold.

Katherine began slipping cups into the sudsy water as Mrs. James pulled a large dishtowel from a drawer.

"Katherine," she began.

Here it comes. Katherine's hands shook a little, and she had to hold tight to the cup she was rinsing.

"Don't worry Dearie, it isn't anything dreadful." Mrs. James laughed lightly and took the cup from Katherine's trembling hand. "It's only that I've been thinking about how much work this place is—it's very nearly too much even for the two of us now. You know Harold and I have a trip to England coming up later this year, and I do so want you to have some reliable help whilst we're gone. I've been thinking it over the past few days, and I may have thought of a solution."

"And what did your new husband say to your bringing the tea shop along on your honeymoon?" Katherine asked teasingly.

"Oh, he agreed with me that we need another employee. Especially with the trip coming up, but also so I can be home a little more, now that I'm married."

There it was. The nagging something again, prodding her like a child poking at a bruise. Katherine tried to brush it off as she replied, "I know we talked about hiring someone, but who in Harborhaven would be a good fit?"

"That's just it, Dearie." Mrs. James reached up to put a saucer in the cupboard, then turned toward Katherine. "It won't *be* someone from Harborhaven."

"What? Who do you have in mind?"

"I have a cousin of sorts, more like a niece, really. She's in need of a place, rather like you were when you first came to town. I told her we could try it for a while and see how she does."

"That's great!" A wave of relief swept over Katherine, though the nagging something remained.

"Harold's old place is vacant, you know, and we thought she might like to stay there. Of course, I wouldn't dream of asking you to give up your flat upstairs, or to share it with a stranger."

Katherine smiled. "I wouldn't have minded. You've done so much for me, I feel it's only right to try to help someone else in the same boat."

Mrs. James reached over and squeezed Katherine's hand,

suds and all. "I know you wouldn't mind. But Harold's flat will do just fine for her, and it will give her an extra measure of independence, you know."

"I suppose. And what is this cousin's daughter's name?"

"Sally."

"I don't think I've ever known anyone named Sally before."

"Well," Mrs. James said with a chuckle, "If she's anything like she was the last time I saw her, you're in for an adventure."

4

Sally

A rare burst of autumnal sunshine flooded the tall windows which made up the front wall of Miss Harriet's as Katherine wheeled a cart full of clean teacups, napkins and silverware out from the kitchen. She enjoyed the simple routine of setting the tables. It was the last task before opening each morning, and she always tried to get to it early enough to take her time, savoring the simple beauty of precision and order. The outward routine of placing cups and saucers and forks and knives just so settled her, somehow, and gave a sense of peace to what in recent months had become a hectic morning rush.

She had just finished setting the first table when the bell over the door rang and Mrs. James breezed in, followed by a young woman around Katherine's age, with nut-brown hair slicked back into an orderly bun. She wore a tight sort of frozen smile on her round face and her dark brown eyes were wide beneath their long lashes.

"Well, here we are then, my dears. Katherine, this is my cousin Sally. Sally, this is Katherine." Mrs. James gently drew Sally forward as she spoke.

Sally stood hesitantly, clasping her hands before her first one way, then another, as if unsure what to do with them.

"Good to meet you, Sally." Katherine stepped forward and reached out her hand to the newcomer with a friendly smile.

"Me too," was all Sally could manage in reply, but the frozen smile thawed into a genuine one as the two shook hands.

Mrs. James stood to one side, giving the two younger women what Katherine could only describe as a maternal smile. "Katherine, I thought Sally could shadow you today, and maybe get a feel for how we do things before we decide on her specific duties."

"That sounds like a good plan." Katherine said. Turning to Sally, she motioned towards the cart. "I was just setting the tables. I'll show you."

Mrs. James moved off toward the kitchen with her usual graceful gait, while Katherine and Sally began laying out the forks and knives at the next empty table. As they worked, Katherine stole a glance at her new coworker. She was neatly attired in a straight black skirt and white blouse, sleeves buttoned tightly at the wrist. Unlike her graceful cousin, Sally moved clumsily on thick-soled black shoes, dressy but practical for the all-day walking and standing her new job would entail.

"Have you ever worked in a tearoom before?" Katherine asked cheerfully, setting out a cup and saucer.

"No..." Sally's face clouded a little. "I've worked lots of places, but never a tearoom." Katherine noticed an accent, similar to Mrs. James' but different. Rounder, somehow.

"And are you from the same part of England as your cousin?"

"A bit northward... I don't suppose you'd know the place if I told you."

Katherine smiled, "No, I suppose not... I have to admit I haven't paid too much attention to the geography of Great Britain. Do you have brothers or sisters?"

"Yes, quite a few..." Sally's voice trailed and she turned quickly towards the cart, bumping the table and causing all the dishes to rattle as she did. "Oh, I'm sorry." She turned around just as quickly to help set everything back in its place again, this time bumping the cart in her hurry. "I'm ever so clumsy. I really will try to be more careful."

"It's all right, Sally." Katherine said gently. She recognized in the younger woman signs of the same deep, unsettled hurt she herself had exhibited when she first arrived at Miss Harriet's. Her heart immediately warmed to Sally. *How can I help you?* she wondered silently, watching as the thick-soled shoes careened their owner to the next table, tripping slightly over themselves on the way.

* * * *

"You know," Rosie whispered, catching Katherine by the arm. "I'm concerned for Miss Harriet."

Katherine stifled a heavy sigh. The lunch rush was in full swing, and Miss Harriet, or rather, Mrs. James, was in the kitchen, replenishing their supply of scones and Cornish pasties. "Oh really?"

"Yes. I know she's kindhearted, but..." Rosie let her sentence trail as she nodded her head significantly across the room to where Sally was fumbling her way through clearing the table.

"Rosie, it's her first day." Katherine could feel the irritation growing in her like an expanding balloon.

"I know that, but have you *seen* how clumsy she is?" A clatter rang out and Sally dropped to her knees, hurriedly gathering up the bin of silverware she had knocked off her cart.

With a warning look at Rosie, Katherine walked quickly over to help.

"Here, let me." she said gently.

"I don't know what happens sometimes, I just can't seem to keep from dropping things."

Sally tried to laugh, but Katherine noticed a deep red flush creep over the new girl's face. She put a hand on Sally's shoulder and smiled. "You know, it's only your first day. You're probably just nervous."

Sally reached for the last fork and stood to put the bin back on the cart. Then with a hurried, "Thank you, Katherine." Sally wheeled the cart into the kitchen.

"See what I mean?" Rosie said as Katherine passed her table again.

"Now, Rosie, you leave Sally alone. It certainly doesn't make settling into a new job easier to have someone watching to find fault with you."

"*Me*? Finding fault? Why—"

Katherine turned deliberately and walked into the kitchen.

She always found Rosie irritating, but today—today it went beyond irritation. This was anger: a seething, burning anger that made her want to unleash a torrent of bitter words on Rosie, to make her feel what the victims of her gossip felt. After all, hadn't her insinuations driven away many of the Harborside's customers when Captain Braddock first returned to run the shop? And now, to pick on someone like Sally, trying so hard to do her best—it was too much.

"Katherine, what's wrong?" Mrs. James asked, pulling a tray of fragrant scones from the oven and sliding another in.

"Tell me again why we have to put up with that woman?" Katherine's tone held more force than she had intended to let out.

"Ah, Rosie's been at it again, I see." Setting her tray down, Mrs. James turned. "Sally, this will be good for you to hear as well."

Sally froze, holding a handful of forks mid-air above the bin she had been replenishing.

"For all her faults, Rosie is one of our most loyal customers. She says more than she ought most days, and that's certainly not right. But if it were you, wouldn't you want others to treat *you* with kindness and longsuffering? Whatever it is she has said today, let it motivate you to look beyond her words to her heart. For all her flash and bluster, she's a very lonely woman. She tears others down, seeking to build herself up. Like everyone else in the world, she simply wants to be loved."

All was silent in the kitchen for a moment, until one of Sally's forks slipped from her grasp and clattered to the floor.

Mrs. James put a hand on Katherine's shoulder. "I can see

that some solitude might be in order, Katherine, before you go back out, so I'll take over for you while you finish up in here. The last scones are in, and those pasties are ready to be plated." Turning at the doorway, Mrs. James said gently, "and remember, Katherine, 'what doth the Lord require of thee'?"

"To do justly, and to love mercy, and to walk humbly with thy God," Katherine answered quoting a verse they had recently been discussing. "Thank you," Katherine said with a faint smile as Mrs. James moved towards the doorway and a wide-eyed Sally followed her with the cart.

Lord, help me. Katherine prayed, letting out a long breath, lifting up her anger and bitterness to the Lord, even as her hands moved about the mundane necessities of scones and pasties and tea trays.

5

Rainy Day at the Harborside

"Thou wilt shew me the path of life: in Thy presence is fulness of joy; at Thy right hand there are pleasures for evermore."

Katherine sat in her window seat, curled up in a blanket, Bible on her lap. As she gazed out at the roofs of the buildings across the street, she drank in the stillness of the moment. The window, studded with raindrops, the dark sky just beginning to take on a lighter shade of dull grey, the sun's silent rising behind the heavy curtain of clouds, each seemed to echo the joyful quiet in her heart. Katherine read the verse again and took a deep breath, savoring it all.

This morning, she *felt* the verse to be true. She had learned to spend time with God, and found joy in His presence like nothing she had ever known before. But as much as she wanted to sit and bask in the joy and peace and quiet rest, snuggled beneath a blanket with the raindrops tapping against the glass, she knew she needed to get up. Today was Thursday, the day she unpacked boxes and restocked shelves at the Harborside.

As she reluctantly moved the blanket aside and walked over to the coatrack by the door, Katherine heard muffled sounds of baking sheets and mixing bowls. *Mrs. James must be here.* She bent to pull on her boots. Then, as she pulled a jacket on over her thick sweater, she heard a crash. It sounded as if someone had dropped a whole stack of baking sheets, all at once. *Sally must be here too.*

She threw a scarf around her neck and pulled a warm hat over her dark brown curls. The weather had finally turned, and she knew it would be a wet, cold walk across Harborhaven's downtown blocks to the Harborside this morning.

As she came downstairs into the tearoom, she saw Sally carefully laying forks and knives and dishes on the tables. She bent close to the tablecloth, adjusting each piece three or four times before moving on to the next. Katherine smiled at her thoroughness.

"Good morning, Sally!"

The girl jumped, disturbing the silverware she had just carefully placed. "Oh, good morning, Katherine. I'm supposed to try waiting tables today, since you won't be here."

"That's great, Sally! And do you feel any less nervous today?"

"A little... although I did still knock the pans off the kitchen counter."

"I heard," Katherine chuckled. "But I'm sure it will get better in time."

Sally gave her a skeptical look. "Did you drop things when you first started?"

Katherine paused a moment, thinking. "No, at least not often... but everyone's different.

Sally's face clouded a little as she repeated softly, "Yes, everyone is different."

Katherine didn't know what to say next, and there was an awkward silence for a moment as Sally bent back over the table and put even more scrupulous care into arranging the forks and spoons and knives before her.

"Well, I'm going to say good morning to Mrs. James before I leave."

Sally didn't look up. "Ok."

Katherine walked over to the kitchen doorway, pulled the curtain to one side and peeked her head in. "Good morning!"

"Ah! Good morning, Dearie. Want anything for the road? There's a batch of cheddar scones fresh from the oven."

"That's perfect, Thanks!" Katherine grinned as Mrs. James wrapped a hot scone in a napkin and handed it to her. "What would I do if I didn't live above a tea shop?"

Mrs. James chuckled. "Why, you'd just come here for breakfast like everyone else."

"I suppose I would," Katherine replied with a laugh. "See you later."

"Have a good day, Dearie!"

* * * *

"Hello the shop!" Katherine called out as she opened the Harborside's dark green door and stepped inside. She flung her jacket and scarf on the coatrack by the door, took the stiff navy apron off its hook, then turned to survey the shop. The place was permeated with feelings of history and home. Her eyes lingered over the cedar-plank walls, the shelves of tea jars lining one wall, the high counter, the old wood stove, the antique cash register, and the retired sea captain sitting at his desk, hunched over a ledger—all these things added to her cup of joy, and it seemed full, indeed.

"Permission to come aboard?" she leaned against the doorframe of the Captain's Quarters.

Captain Braddock looked up with a weary smile. "I'm sorry, Katherine. I heard you come in, but I was lost in the land of arithmetic calculating this month's sales and couldn't stop till I had finished."

"That's all right," Katherine returned his smile. "Anything you need done in the shop before I begin the unpacking?"

"No, go ahead and get to it." he went back to his ledger. "There's an extra package today."

"An extra package?"

He nodded without looking up, but Katherine caught a telltale flicker of a smile tugging at the corners of his mouth.

Anticipation thrilled through Katherine. This was why she loved unpacking. Opening cargoes from far-off lands always felt like an adventure, and whenever a package came from somewhere new, it was like treading on undiscovered territory.

Taking the inventory clipboard from the wall, Katherine flipped on the lights and descended into the chilly stillness of the storeroom. Just as the captain had said, the box on top of the nearest stack bore a label she didn't recognize.

"Cameroon?" she asked, eyebrows raised, as she noticed Captain Braddock standing in the doorway.

"Yes. Did you know Cameroon has a thriving tea industry?"

"No, I didn't." She took a boxcutter from the wide pocket of her apron and carefully slid the blade between the flaps on either end of the box, then down the seam across the top. Lifting the flaps, Katherine moved the packing material aside and drew out a clear bag full of loose tea. The shriveled-up leaves always reminded her of the grass clippings she used to rake up when her dad mowed their lawn in the Harborhaven summers of long ago.

Looking up at the captain, she tried to keep her expression nonchalant. "Have you tried it yet?"

He stiffened, as if offended. "Of course not. The first cup of a new variety is a family event around here. Always has been, all the way back to the first shipment Captain Jeremiah brought in."

"Well, then," Katherine slowly climbed the steps to hand the bag to the captain, "It wouldn't do to break tradition." The grin she had been holding back spread across her face, and the captain answered with his own satisfied smile.

"Right, then. Follow me." Captain Braddock led the way across the office to an unobtrusive curtain, which hid the shop's small kitchen. Just then, the bell over the door rang.

Katherine smiled. "I'll go. You make the tea."

Captain Braddock nodded, already filling the kettle with water.

* * * *

When Katherine returned a few minutes later, two cups of steaming liquid sat on the desk, and an extra chair had been placed across from the captain's.

"Customer?" Captain Braddock limped in from the kitchen with a trivet and the pot of tea.

"Yes, they wanted the new Assam we got in last week."

"Ah, yes. That one's been quite popular." There was a short pause as Katherine eyed the cup in front of her.

Finally, he picked up his cup and chuckled. "Go ahead. No sense waiting till it's cold." Katherine raised the cup and smelled the earthy fragrance rising from it. Then she took a sip. Captain Braddock did the same, and for a moment neither spoke.

"Well, what do you think?" Captain Braddock leaned back in his chair and took another sip.

Katherine thought for a moment, trying to put the flavor into words. "It tastes...green. I don't mean like green tea, but ...I don't know, like a forest on a mountain somewhere." She took another sip. "It's very good."

"Well, you're not far off, there, Missy. In a sense, this tea *did* come from a kind of forest on a mountain. The plantation itself is on a high plateau, in the foothills of a volcano. So it does come from a mountainous region, at least. And I suppose you could call a few acres of tea bushes a forest of sorts."

"I did read once about elevation affecting the flavor of tea." Katherine wrapped her fingers around her cup. "How did you find out about this?"

"There are several major tea plantations in Cameroon, see, but they all use the modern crushing and tearing process, which, as you know, utterly destroys the leaves, and the flavor along with it. However, despite their processing methods, Cameroonian tea is known for having a deep color and good taste, so I have been hoping to find a smaller grower that uses a more traditional process.

"I was rummaging in the trunks up in the tower a few weeks ago, and came across some correspondence between my grandmother and a young man in Cameroon who was just getting ready to start planting. That was in the '70s, you see, so I wasn't sure I could find him, but lo and behold—" he paused and raised his teacup—"here we are!"

"So the man's plantation is still there?"

"Yes, which is a bit of a miracle, since it's in an area where there has been much conflict over the years."

Katherine took another sip. "I think this one will do well. It has a deep, mellow flavor." Eyeing the captain warily, she ventured, "I think we should keep this jar on the counter for a while, with a sign, like we did with the silver needle tea last year...just to let people know it's here and where it comes from." Katherine held her breath, knowing how committed Captain Braddock was to relying only on word-of-mouth advertising. That, too, was a Harborside tradition.

"I suppose we might..." Captain Braddock gazed at her with a thoughtful look, as if mulling the idea over. "Now, you and I have work to do, and we'd better get back to it." A bit of his old gruffness returned to his voice as he stood. Then, pouring the last of the tea into their cups, he said with a twinkle in his eye, "Better take that with you. The storeroom's a mite chilly today."

* * * *

When Katherine returned to Miss Harriet's that evening, she found Mrs. James alone in the kitchen, filling the sink with water. She looked up as Katherine entered.

"Hello, Dearie. Good day at the Harborside?"

"Yes. We got a new tea in from Cameroon. I think it will make a good addition to our menu. Where's Sally?"

The older woman gave a weary sigh. "I sent her home. It had been a long day, and I could tell she was tired."

Katherine eyed her friend. "Things didn't go well today, did they?"

"They could have gone worse..." Mrs. James managed a half-smile.

"Ah." Katherine picked up a dishtowel. "You wash, I'll dry."

Mrs. James smiled appreciatively, then began loading the sink with fragile china dishes. They worked in silence for a while before Mrs. James stopped, looked up at the ceiling and said, "I don't know what to do."

Katherine silently waited, knowing her friend well enough to recognize when she just needed to talk her problems out.

"I mean, that stack of baking trays this morning was just the beginning. She dropped three tea trays—thankfully empty, but they make such a clatter spilled her bin of silverware several times, and knocked an *entire* jampot into Rosie's lap."

Katherine stifled a giggle.

"I keep telling myself it's only her second day, and maybe I pushed her into serving tables too soon... I just don't know how to help her."

Katherine set her dishtowel on the counter and put an

arm around the older woman's shoulders. Mrs. James leaned her head against Katherine's and let out a deep breath. "Thank you, Katherine. You always know when I need space to chatter."

"Can I tell you something that might help?" Katherine said, as the two went back to their washing and drying.

"Of course, Dearie."

"Well, yesterday when I was so upset at Rosie...she had been picking at Sally.—Behind her back, of course, but you know how she is. It may be that she said something to or about Sally in her hearing that unnerved her more than usual."

Mrs. James looked thoughtfully into the soap bubbles for a moment. "Yes, that could be. I'll have to keep an eye on that. In the meantime, what should we do with Sally tomorrow?"

Katherine swiped her dishtowel around the inside of a delicate teacup for a moment as she thought. "I think we should give her a few select tables, people who will be patient with her—Mrs. Penelope and Mr. Patten, for instance—and have her bus tables and fill trays the rest of the day. That way she gets experience without feeling so overwhelmed."

"That's a good idea, Katherine." Mrs. James' eyes lit up. "And I can work on teaching her the art of presentation. She might like the behind-the-scenes work of putting the orders together."

"Yes, I think she would." Katherine nodded. "But whatever we do, let's be sure to keep her away from Rosie."

"Agreed."

6

A Tempest in the
Tearoom

"Uh...Welcome to Miss Harriet's...um... what do you want?"

Katherine winced as she listened to Sally talk to the couple at the next table. *We'll have to work on that.*

Hand-picking her tables had really helped, but she could tell Sally was still struggling. Instead of the quiet clinking of delicate china cups and saucers and the gentle hum of hushed conversations, days at Miss Harriet's were now punctuated with crashes, rattles and Sally's inimitable "Oh! Sorry!" as she tripped and stumbled and fumbled through her duties.

It was more than just clumsiness, though. Katherine could sense something deeper—an unsettled uncertainty of heart, perhaps a pain hidden inside—that kept her from focusing on the tasks at hand. And Katherine could relate. Not long ago, she had gone about her days nursing a secret pain of her own.

She knew that Sally needed to find for herself the "old paths" of relationship with God that had brought true rest to Katherine's soul. But she also knew that Sally had to choose those paths for herself. Mrs. James had helped Katherine find them. How she wished she could do the same for Sally!

"Oh! You *clumsy* girl...just *look* what you've done!"

Katherine wheeled around, startled out of her thoughts by the shrill cry of a voice raised to a pitch unusual for even the excitable Rosie.

The large woman sat with ruffled hair, frantically dabbing at her extravagant hat with a napkin. Sally stood frozen, as if caught between fear and indignation. Mrs. James was out of the kitchen in a flash, a kitchen towel and soothing tone at the ready.

"Now, what's the matter, Rosie? Has your hat met with an accident of some kind?"

"Accident! You call dumping an entire pitcher of water all over it an accident?"

"An *entire* pitcher? Let me see." Mrs. James examined the hat, then said, "Well, now, it doesn't look as bad as all that. I do believe it will be right as rain once it has a chance to dry a little. Would you like me to take it and set it somewhere safe while you finish your tea?"

"No." Rosie glared at Sally, who had retreated a step or two from the table. "That girl would probably just dump another pitcher on it when I wasn't looking."

Mrs. James' tone held an edge of firmness as she replied. "Now, Rosie. I know you're upset about your hat, but if it's just water, it will dry out all right. See? It's beginning to look better all ready."

Rosie rose angrily to her feet. "No. It's ruined for sure. just like this establishment will be, if you persist in employing such incompetent staff. I know you're soft-hearted, Miz Harriet, but I never knew you were such a *fool*."

At this, Sally burst forward, fists clenched, eyes flashing. "Now you just *shut it*! Here's the kindest woman you'll ever meet, and you go sayin' nasty things about her just because I spilled a little water on your ugly old hat."

For one terrible moment, Katherine thought the two might break out into a physical fight, but Mrs. James stepped up to Sally and laid a firm but gentle hand on her arm.

"Thank you, Sally, dear, but that's all we'll have of that." She turned and looked Sally directly in the eyes. "Go back to the kitchen now. I'll be along presently."

Sally clumped off to the kitchen, pausing to throw one last smoldering glare at Rosie before disappearing behind the curtain.

Feeling vindicated, Rosie stood a little straighter and opened her mouth to speak, but Mrs. James turned to her with an icy calmness Katherine had never seen before.

"As for you, Rosie. I'll thank you not to come around here insulting my staff and causing a scene. I think it's time for you to go home." Then, with a polite smile, she handed Rosie her purse and said, "Tea's on us today."

Rosie frowned, grabbed her purse, smashed the offended hat onto her head, opened her mouth and shut it again several times in a way that reminded Katherine of a perplexed fish, then stomped out the door, huffing and puffing as she went.

Silence reigned in the tearoom till Mrs. James, turning to address the roomful of stunned customers, smoothed her apron and said lightly, "Ever so sorry about the interruption. Please, carry on." Then, nodding to Katherine, Mrs. James walked calmly into the kitchen.

A spontaneous applause broke out as soon as she was out of sight, and Katherine couldn't help but chuckle a little. Apparently, she wasn't the only one happy to see Rosie get taken down a peg or two.

* * * *

"That was magnificent. I've never seen anything like it," Katherine overheard one man say as she passed by his table a few minutes later.

"Such restraint!" said the woman sitting across from him. "I would have slapped the old busybody." Then, stopping Katherine, she said in a softer tone, "Your young friend will be all right, won't she? That horrid woman was so rude."

"I'm sure she will be fine," Katherine said, "Thank you for asking, though."

* * * *

Sally kept to the kitchen the rest of the day, and Katherine didn't see much of her until closing. It touched her deeply to hear table after table of guests ask after Sally, even though she had only been working at the shop for a short while. Stories of "the incident" as the locals had begun to call it, circulated quickly through the town, as any bit of gossip did.

But instead of painting Rosie as the victim, Sally was dubbed the sweet, ill-used girl who had the pluck to stand up to her assailant. She was the underdog, suddenly "one of us," instantly made part of Harborhaven once and for all. And just as instantly, Rosie became the official villain of Harborhaven. Mrs. James, however, earned a place as the town hero, an object of majestic awe to be whispered about in corners and beamed upon when present.

It took an effort to keep cheerful and professional, to focus on what needed to be done, when all Katherine wanted to do was run back to the kitchen and see how Sally fared. Finally, she saw the last customers out and flipped the sign to *"Come Again Soon."*

Letting out a deep sigh she had been holding in all afternoon, she went to the kitchen door and gingerly peeked around the curtain.

"Hullo." Sally's voice was quiet as she ran water into the sink to begin the washing-up.

"Hi." Katherine slipped on a dishwashing apron and joined the younger woman at the sink. "Where's Mrs. James?"

"She stepped out for a bit to get dinner ready at home."

"Oh." Katherine couldn't decide how to broach the question she most wanted to ask.

"We've had a good talk, she and I." Sally ventured, as if reading Katherine's thoughts.

"That's good." Katherine felt a wave of relief wash over her heart. She smiled. "I'll wash, you dry."

Sally smiled and reached for a dishtowel. "I knew it was wrong how I acted, but I felt I couldn't stop myself."

"I know. I've felt that way about Rosie myself."

"You have?" Sally's eyes grew wide. "What did you do?"

"I prayed." Katherine said simply, easing a teapot into the soapy water.

"And...did it help?"

"Yeah. It did," Katherine nodded. "I *didn't* pour a pot of tea all over her, so I guess it worked all right."

Sally grinned. "I guess that did work."

The two giggled, then Sally grew serious again.

"May I ask you a question?—No strings attached, I promise."

"Sure."

"Do you, I mean..." she paused, as if searching for the right words. "All that about prayer and church and the Bible. You both talk about it all the time, but... is it... is it *real?*"

A broad smile broke out on Katherine's face. "Yes, Sally, it's real. It's the realest thing that ever was, and it can be real for you too, if you want it to be.

Sally shook her head. "No, I'm not religious... I never was."

"Neither am I." Katherine said, handing Sally another cup.

"What?" Sally raised her eyebrows.

"Religion is all about what I can *do* to appease God or to get what I want from Him. That's not what Christianity is about at all."

"It isn't?" Sally's brows bunched together into a puzzled frown.

"Not at all. The Bible says that it's by grace we are saved, through faith. I can't ever be or do enough good to *earn* salvation, but the gift of salvation makes me want to do good because I love God, who loves me and who forgave my sin. So you see, I don't do the things I do or live the way I live because I'm religious, I do them because I'm *forgiven*."

Sally looked at Katherine for a long while, then began drying the cup in her hand. "Forgiven..." she said to herself.

Lord, help her see. Katherine prayed as the two worked on

in silence. Finally, Sally looked up and said, I think there's a cake plate yet," and went out into the tearoom to get it.

As she returned, Katherine said,

"Sally... can I ask you a question—no strings attached?"

"Sure."

"Was that jampot yesterday entirely accidental?"

Sally's eyes twinkled mischievously as she replied slowly, "Well... maybe not *entirely*."

7

An Apprentice

"D'you think she'll show?" Sally's eyes were wide as she asked the question Katherine herself had pondered all morning.

"I don't know. Rosie's been coming here every day for so long—I honestly can't imagine what she would do all day without Miss Harriet's." Katherine placed a cup and saucer on the table they were setting.

Sally's face darkened, her shoulders trembling as she drew in a long breath.

Katherine put her hand on the girl's arm. "Sally, if she does come today, I don't think she'll say a word to you. In fact, she'll probably ignore the fact that you exist, just to spare her own ego."

"Katherine's right, you know. It's her way." Mrs. James came through the kitchen doorway carrying a baking tray full of scones for the counter display. "She won't want to admit she's had her pride wounded. She'll likely just sit somewhere prominent doing her best to look like an innocent victim. It's not right, but there it is." She set the tray down and leaned forward over the counter, fixing her eyes on the two young ladies. "Our job is to be kind, whatever she might say or do. *Kind*, you hear?" There was a rare note of firmness in her voice that startled Katherine.

"Yes'm." Sally blurted, almost involuntarily, as Katherine nodded in silence.

The older woman straightened up again and took a breath. "Now that's settled, let's get on with our morning. Sounds like a stormy walk for you, Katherine. That wind's been howling in off the harbor all night, and the rain's been pouring."

"Don't worry. I bundled up extra this morning," Katherine grinned. "But it *would* be nice to have something warm to keep my fingers from getting too cold as I walk."

Mrs. James chuckled. "I may have just the thing. I'll be right back."

Katherine walked over to where Sally was busily setting tables and got to work while she waited.

"Does Auntie H. always send you off with a snack?"

"Usually." Katherine chuckled. "Auntie H...it's funny to hear her called that."

Sally blushed, "My mum would be horrified. She always insisted we call her *Aunt Harriet*, in all capitals, like, but my brother and I, we always called her Auntie H. between the two of us." She laid down a butter knife and turned towards the cart as she continued. "Then when mum got sick, and then... when she was gone... we just sort of kept calling her Auntie H. since there was no one to care."

"Are you and your brother close still?"

"No. He's gone too." As Sally returned to the table with a handful of napkins, Katherine could see her eyes shimmering with tears. For a moment, she thought Sally was going to tell her more, but instead, she turned with an abrupt, "I'd better get on with this." and moved the cart to the other side of the room.

"Here we are, Dearie. Just the thing for a cold morning." Mrs. James held out a small bundle wrapped in a napkin.

Katherine gently lifted a corner of the napkin and peeked inside at the half-circle pocket of pastry, sealed along the edge with a fancy braid, its hot filling sending up trails of fragrant steam.

"You have the pasties done early today! Could you spare one more for the captain? He likes your pasties—though don't tell him I told you." Katherine winked.

"Of course. I'd be glad to send him one."

"Who's the captain?" Sally asked as Mrs. James walked back into the kitchen.

"He's the owner of the Harborside—you know, the shop I work at on the days I'm not here."

"Oh." Sally adjusted a fork before moving on to the next table. Looking up with a frown, she asked, "Why doesn't he like people to know he likes pasties?"

Katherine chuckled. "I suppose it's because he likes people to think he's a gruff old curmudgeon, but he's actually very nice once you get to know him."

Sally raised her eyebrows. "That's strange."

"It sounds stranger than it is," Katherine said with a grin. "Actually, I think you'd like him, and the Harborside. Maybe we can talk your 'Auntie H.' into sending you over to fetch the tea order sometime this week."

Sally's eyes lit up. "I'd like that!"

"I know that look." Mrs. James returned from the kitchen with a small tin, which she handed to Katherine. "For the captain, with my compliments... I happened to make extra this morning." Turning to Sally, she smiled and asked, "Now, what is it you two were just planning?"

"Katherine was telling me about the Harborside. Can I go see it?"

"I thought she and I might fetch the tea order tomorrow," Katherine interjected.

"That sounds like a very good idea! Let's plan on it, then." The older lady put an arm around each of the younger two and said, "How glad I am to have you both here!" Then, catching a glimpse of the clock, she pushed Katherine gently towards the door, saying, "Now, we'd better not keep you any longer. We don't want you to be late!"

* * * *

"I hear you had a skirmish at the shop yesterday." Captain Braddock limped over to meet Katherine as she took off her jacket and flung her scarf over her head.

"We did. I still don't know what to think of it..." Handing him the tin, she said casually, "Breakfast. Mrs. James sent them. She said to tell you she made extra this morning."

With a wary look at Katherine, the old man cautiously opened the tin. His eyes widened as a smile slowly spread across his face. "Well, now, that was kind of her." Katherine caught a twinkle in his eye as he set the tin down and limped over to the wood stove, saying "I can't think how she knew I'd like them, though." He stooped down without looking at her and began to poke discerningly at the fire.

Katherine sighed. There was no getting around the captain. "I may have just mentioned..." she let her voice trail.

Captain Braddock looked up with a grin. "I kinda figured so. Well, I'm grateful, however it came about. Those are quite the treat." Straightening up with a slight grimace, he shut the door of the old wood stove and turned to face Katherine. "This weather's not too good on my old bones." Crossing to the large shop window, he tugged deftly at the dark green rolling blind and eased it up.

"I suppose it won't be too good for business, either." Katherine said, joining him at the window and peering out into the dim gloom outside.

"I suppose not. Tea?"

Katherine nodded. Slow cozy days like today were just the kind of days she liked at the Harborside.

* * * *

The two had just settled into their chairs in the Captain's quarters, when the bell over the door gave a sharp, cheerful jingle.

"Cap'n, are ya here?" A little boy blustered through the doorway before Katherine and the captain could even rise to greet their young customer.

"That I am, young man. What brings you here so early?"

"Mom wanted me to give you this." He thrust a piece of paper towards the captain.

"What is it, Tommy?" he gave the boy a bewildered look.

"You have to *read* it, of course!" Tommy chuckled.

Captain Braddock held the paper up and squinted at it for a moment. Then he looked up at Tommy, who seemed to be holding his breath.

"Let me see if I understand this correctly," he leaned forward. "Your mother doesn't have anyone to watch you after school, and wants to know if we can keep an eye on you here each day, till she gets off work, is that it?"

Tommy nodded, eyes large and pleading.

With a quick look at Katherine, Captain Braddock broke into a grin. "Well, now. I suppose we can find enough around here to keep you busy. When do you want to start coming?"

Tommy let out a rather dramatic sigh of relief. "Mom says I can come tomorrow if you say ok."

"Tomorrow it is," said the captain, with a happy twinkle in his eye. "Now, don't you have to get off to school? You wouldn't want to be late, now would you?"

"No, Sir." Tommy gave a little salute. "See you tomorrow!"

Katherine watched him bounce out the door, then looked over at the captain. Tommy always brought a smile to the old sea captain's face. Having him around more would be good for them all.

"Well, wouldn't you know it, we have an apprentice!" Captain Braddock's voice was soft with wonder, his eyes shining. He shook his head. "Never would have thought there would be a youngster hanging around the shop again."

"Like you used to?"

"Yes, like I used to." He stared out into the shopfront, and Katherine recognized the familiar faraway look in his eyes as he remembered the days when the Harborside had bustled with Braddocks.

"I'll just get started on the jars." Katherine quietly stood and drained the last of her tea. She grabbed a dust rag from behind the counter and walked to the wall of shelves on the opposite end of the shop. *Maybe having Tommy around will help the captain not feel so alone.*

* * *

"Well, what happened?" Katherine asked as she let herself into the tearoom after closing that night and found Sally in the kitchen washing the dishes.

"Just what Auntie H. said would happen. She came, sat with a ridiculous fake look on her face, and made sure everyone saw her act as if I didn't exist." Sally said, curling her lip in disgust. "I don't know how Auntie H. puts up with the old peacock."

Katherine shook her head. "Sometimes I wonder that, too. But Rosie hasn't always been this way. In fact, before now, she's only been dramatic and ridiculous, never really malicious. It makes me wonder if something has happened to make her so sour all of a sudden."

"Sour's the word," Sally said, shaking her head.

"How did everything else go today?" Katherine asked, picking up a dishtowel and starting to dry the teacups Sally had placed on the drying mat.

"Fine." Sally shrugged. "Auntie H had me assembling trays

most of the day, though I did bus tables as well. There weren't too many people today."

"We didn't have many at the Harborside either," Looking up, she added, "It's the rain. It keeps people indoors, though the locals should all be used to it by now." She leaned towards Sally and whispered, "But I'll tell you a secret—I like the rainy days the best."

"Me too." Sally said, "Reminds me of home." She studied her dishrag for a moment, a faraway look in her eyes. Then, forgetting to rinse a plate before handing it to Katherine, she suddenly asked, "How did you start working there? At the Harborside, I mean."

"Well," Katherine reached over to rinse the plate herself. "When I first came back, your aunt gave me a job and a place to stay, and I was happy here. But one day, she sent me to the Harborside to pick up some tea, and as soon as I walked through the door it felt like home, somehow. Captain Braddock and I got along well enough, and he could tell I was fascinated by the history of the place, so he hired me on as his assistant."

Sally had stopped washing altogether, staring out the little window above the sink. "Do you suppose..." she began, turning her wistful eyes towards Katherine.

"Yes?"

"Do you suppose everyone has somewhere like that, somewhere that's *home*?"

Katherine picked up another cup and rubbed it thoughtfully with her dishcloth. "I don't know for sure... but it only seems right that everyone would have somewhere they feel they belong. But..." she took a breath, not sure if this was the right time. *Lord, help me to have the words!* she prayed silently.

"Did I ever tell you why I came back to Harborhaven?"

Sally shook her head as she handed Katherine a saucer, this time remembering to rinse the suds off.

"Well, you know that I grew up here, right?"

"Yes, I think you mentioned it."

"When I was only nine, we moved away and life changed drastically. I loved my home here, our life here as a family. The new house was in the city. It was dark, dirty, and lonely. We moved because my dad lost his job, and although he found a new job, it didn't pay nearly what he used to make. My mom ended up working too, to help pay the bills, and even though I knew she had to, I still felt abandoned. From the day we moved, I never felt at home again."

"Till the Harborside."

"Right."

Sally looked up as Katherine paused. "So what did you do?"

"I ran away, to the place that felt like home. Not right then, of course, but when I finished college I came back, expecting everything to be the same."

Sally's face clouded. "But it wasn't."

Katherine shook her head. "No, and if it weren't for your aunt, I would have ended up wandering aimlessly, always searching for something that felt like home, but knowing things would never go back the way they were."

"So what happened? I mean, I know you stayed here, but what happened to make it home?"

"Part of it was your aunt's kindness, her constant peace

and joy. It helped point me to the one thing that could make a difference."

"And what was that?"

"The old paths."

Sally's face wrinkled with confusion. "The *what*?"

"I suppose it doesn't make much sense when I put it like that." She wiped a plate dry as she collected her thoughts.

"Soon after I came here, your aunt and I were sitting in church and the pastor read a verse from Jeremiah. It said, 'Stand ye in the ways, and see, and ask for the old paths, where is the good way and walk therein, and ye shall find rest for your souls.'

"That phrase, 'rest for your souls' stuck with me. That was what I had been looking for all along, a place where my soul would finally feel at rest, like it had in those lovely childhood days at home. Your aunt helped me understand that the 'old paths' were simply the things the Bible teaches about having a relationship with God. So, I started praying and reading the Bible and getting to know God."

"And did it work?"

Katherine couldn't help but beam. Her heart felt it would overflow with the truth of her answer. "Yes, it did work. It took time, and I had to let go in some areas in my life where I was holding onto bitterness and unforgiveness, but yes, God has given me rest for my soul." She lifted a stack of cups into a cupboard before continuing. "Of course, life has its ups and downs, and I can't say my emotions always feel at rest, but whatever comes, whether it's early mornings or getting caught in a downpour—"

"or Rosie?" Sally interjected.

"Or even Rosie." Katherine chuckled. "Whatever there is going on in my life, underneath it all, there is a sense of rest, of having Someone I can always go to, a refuge, a home, a family." She turned to face the younger woman. "Sally, I've come to realize that my longings for home, for a place to belong, for people to belong to, those are just the surface of a deeper longing, a longing that home and family can never fill. You will never find true rest from those longings until you get close to God."

Sally was quiet for a long while, and Katherine began to wonder whether she had said too much, or too little. But she sensed that God had helped her with her words, and while the two worked in silence, Katherine prayed that whatever was going on in Sally's heart and mind would bring her to the old paths.

8

Adventuring

When Katherine came down the stairs the next morning, she was surprised to see Mr. James sitting at his usual table, with the flowers moved to one side and a fresh pot of tea sending up a fragrant trail of steam.

"Good morning, Katherine! And how are you today?"

"I'm well, thank you." Katherine smiled as she neared his table. "We haven't seen you around here much lately."

Mr. James gave a sheepish grin. "Well, I've been doing a bit more writing from home lately. Harriet made a wonderful little office for me out of a gable room that looking out over her garden and the evergreen trees, with the ocean beyond. She has an instinctive understanding of what makes a good writing space. "

"Good thing you married her, then," Katherine said with a wink.

He chuckled. "Yes, indeed. It certainly is."

Growing suddenly serious, he motioned for her to sit in the chair across from him. As she settled into her chair, Mr. James leaned forward and lowered his voice. "I wanted to ask you, and I trust you to be completely honest: do you think you will be able to manage this place for a few weeks during our trip this winter?"

Katherine thought for a moment. "Yes," she said slowly. "I think so. There will be less tourists then, and I have Sally, although..." she let her voice trail off as she glanced at the curtained doorway, where a low murmur punctuated by the sounds of the mixer and the oven door opening and closing told her both ladies were engrossed in the morning baking.

Mr. James nodded. "I understand." Leaning back in his chair, he looked at Katherine for a moment, eyebrows drawn together in a frown, as if trying to decide how to proceed.

Katherine felt her stomach tighten. *What is it now?*

Finally, Mr. James spoke. "Can I tell you something in confidence?"

Katherine nodded, then swallowed and tried not to hold her breath, her stomach suddenly uneasy.

"I've inherited a house near my sister in New York."

Katherine felt her muscles tense with apprehension.

"Now, don't worry. We're not moving there. I do intend to keep the place, though. Harriet and I looked it over while we were there on our honeymoon, and she thinks it will be good to have someplace to stay when we visit my sister."

Katherine took a breath. "Well, I suppose congratulations are in order." She watched Mr. James straighten in his chair, and sensed this wasn't all.

"That brings me to why I wanted to talk to you." Leaning

forward again, he folded his hands on the table. "I know this place is a lot to handle, and I know Sally is still getting settled, which probably adds to the load somewhat. I'd like to take Harriet to spend a week in New York just before our trip to England, since we fly from there anyway. It's not for sure yet, but we plan to fly Sally out towards the end of that week, in time for New Year's Eve, which may mean a day or two of going it on your own here."

"Just a day or two shouldn't be too much." She managed a smile, though her mind was whirling.

The reporter leaned forward and gave her a scrutinizing look. "I don't doubt your capability—Harriet says you did a stellar job while we were away. But I want you to promise to tell Harriet or me if this place becomes too much of a burden. It is Harriet's tea shop, after all, and we both view it as her responsibility, not yours. "

Katherine nodded.

"Do you promise to tell us if it becomes overwhelming?"

"Yes. I promise."

"Good." Straightening up in his chair, he smiled suddenly. "Now, would you like a cup of tea?"

* * * *

Later that morning, Sally and Katherine were working to clear and set several tables in preparation for the lunch rush. Looking over at Mrs. James, who was sitting with her husband at his usual table by the window, Sally suddenly nudged Katherine and asked in a low voice,

"D'you suppose she dresses to match the tearoom, or did she decorate the tearoom the way she dresses?"

Katherine chuckled, noticing how her employer's floral skirt coordinated with the flowers on the tables. "Maybe some of both. I suppose it's partly just her personality coming through." They finished laying out the silverware and pushed the cart to the next table.

As they cleared the dishes, Katherine asked, "Did you know her mother?"

"Yes, we called her Gran, though she wasn't our gran any more than Auntie H. was our aunt. We used to stay with her sometimes in the summer."

"Then you saw her flower garden?"

"Oh, yes. It was just a little space, but she had it jam-packed with plants. She sure loved her flowers, Gran did."

"I've always wondered if that's why your aunt surrounds herself with flowers. Perhaps they remind her of her mother."

Sally looked over at Mrs. James, her dark eyes widening. "I never thought of that. I suppose they do."

Just then, the bell over the door gave a violent ring, and Rosie blew in, letting in a gust of chilly wind from the blustery outdoors. She stood for a moment, holding her hat protectively with one hand, before banging the door closed with the other.

Sally leaned over to Katherine and whispered, "What an entrance. Does she ever just *walk* through a doorway like normal people?"

Katherine shook her head, and the two stifled a giggle. Nudging Sally with her elbow, she started to move the cart to the kitchen. "Come on, Let's get this cart unloaded."

Looking over her shoulder, Katherine saw Mrs. James still engrossed in conversation with her husband. The nagging something rose in her heart again, and she turned back to the cart, trying to push away the little prick of pain she couldn't quite identify.

* * * *

"Well, girls, I think it's safe to say that the lunch rush is well and truly over. You've both worked so hard today, and I know you'll want to visit awhile with Captain Braddock, so why don't you both take the rest of the afternoon off?"

Sally broke into a smile brighter than any Katherine had seen so far. "Truly?" she asked.

"Truly, darling Sally." Mrs. James responded, wrapping her niece in a big hug. "By the way," she added, "I thought you handled your tables quite well today."

A pink blush spread over Sally's face as she ducked her head and said, "Katherine helped me figure out what to say, and it helped a lot."

"I'll say!" Katherine was happy to be able to add her own sincere praise. "Mrs. Penelope has quite taken to you. She told me today that she's becoming very fond of 'that dear girl who brings the scones.'"

Another wave of pink spread over Sally's face.

"Well, Dearies, let's not stand here all day. You've got the rest of the afternoon to go off adventuring, although I do wish it weren't quite so stormy out."

"That's all right." Katherine took a paper from her apron pocket. "Stormy days are the best kind for an adventure to the Harborside. Let me just double-check my list and we'll get going."

* * * *

Before long, the two young ladies had bundled up in coats, scarves, and hats and ventured out into the blustering wind and rain that swept in off the harbor.

"This way." Katherine said, leading Sally down Main Street.

The tall Victorian brick of the downtown blocks sheltered them from the wind and rain, but strong gusts still whipped down the side streets, ambushing them at each street corner, tugging at their scarves and jackets.

Katherine paused at the corner of First Street and almost had to shout over the noise of the storm as she pointed to the long flight of stairs that connected Harborhaven's downtown to the neighborhood of Cliffton above.

"That's where I used to live, up there. I'll take you sometime."

Sally nodded, pulling her jacket tighter as they crossed the street and trudged onwards.

Soon, they reached the last historic block of downtown Harborhaven, and Katherine led Sally down the length of the rectangular brick warehouse.

"This whole thing used to belong to the Harborside." Katherine said, "But now it's just the shop at the far end. We're almost there."

"Good." Sally said, "I think my jacket's nearly soaked through."

* * * *

The two hurried into the shop and Katherine quickly closed the door against the wind and rain. Sally looked up. "Do all the shops here have a bell?"

Katherine chuckled. "Yes, but this bell's special."

Sally frowned. "How?"

"This bell has a story. I'll tell you about it later, though. Let's get these jackets off and go find the captain."

The two helped each other peel off their dripping coats and scarves, and Katherine hung them up on the coatrack.

"Captain," she called out, "Where are you? I've brought Sally with me."

There was a creak overhead, and a deep muffled voice. "He must be upstairs," Katherine said, leading the way to the spiral staircase in the corner. Turning at the bottom of the stairs, she saw Sally, still gazing around the room, trying to take it all in.

"Katherine, come on up, and bring yer friend with you."

Sally's eyes grew even wider as she reached the top of the staircase. They stood in an octagonal room with large round windows all around, and a big sea chest at the base of every window. Katherine turned to watch her friend's reaction, and chuckled at her wide eyes and stammered surprise.

"But...but, why didn't I see this when we were walking over?"

"A trick of architecture." Captain Braddock said, getting up with difficulty from where he had been kneeling by one of the sea chests. Limping over to Sally, he held out a hand. "Captain Braddock. And you must be Sally?"

"Yes," Sally said, shaking his hand with a guarded smile.

"Well, what do you think of the view?" Katherine asked, gesturing towards the windows overlooking the stormy harbor.

"It's..." her voice trailed off as she stared out at the storm. "I can see why we got so wet on the way here."

Captain Braddock turned to look at Katherine, his bushy eyebrows raised. "Well, now. What am I thinking? Here I am keeping you up here where it's cold when you two have just been out in the wind and rain. Let's get you downstairs and I'll make some tea." Glancing at Sally, he leaned toward Katherine. "Pu-erh Sheng?"

Katherine grinned. "Yes, I think that will be just right."

"What are you talking about?" Sally asked with a puzzled frown.

"You'll see." Katherine called over her shoulder as she started down the spiral staircase.

* * * *

The storm had cleared by the time Katherine and Sally walked back across the downtown blocks to Miss Harriet's, but an uncertain haze of grey still hung in the sky.

"I'm glad to see you're back before dark," Mrs. James said as they came through the door. "Did you enjoy your adventure?"

Sally nodded. "We got drenched on our way over. But Captain Braddock gave us the most wonderful tea I've ever tasted, and let us sit by the wood stove to get warm again. Oh, and when we first got there, we watched the storm from the little room at the top of the staircase."

Mrs. James raised her eyebrows. "You went into the room at the top of the staircase?"

"Yes, and we could see waves crashing in the harbor."

"Captain Braddock must be mellowing with his years," Mrs. James said.

"Yes," Katherine leaned over and explained to Sally, "I didn't get to see that room until I had been here almost a year, and your aunt has never seen it."

"Then I wonder why he let me come up there?"

Katherine shrugged, trying to brush off the unease tugging at her heart. "I don't know. Sometimes the captain can be very private and reserved, but he also has an instinct about people. He must have thought you were the right kind of person."

"Well, I'm glad, anyway," Sally said, flashing another wide grin.

"Now, girls," Mrs. James gave a sudden little clap. "Since you're back, how about some help with the dishes?"

* * * *

After the dishes were done and the other two ladies had gone home, Katherine opened the door to her apartment and stepped inside. Dropping the keys into a bowl on the table by the door, she looked over at the pool of dim blue light streaming in through the window.

Crossing the dark room, she curled up on the window seat with a pillow in her arms. The nagging something had returned that day, and it wasn't just fear of change. It was time. She needed to face whatever it was head-on instead of pushing it back into a corner of her heart.

Leaning her head against the cool windowpane, she closed her eyes. *Lord, what is it? Show me, please?* She opened her eyes and hugged the pillow tighter. She thought of seeing Mrs. James and her husband deep in conversation, and remembered the sting of—was it jealousy? Not quite.

At the Harborside, as she watched Sally experience the beauty and wonder of the little shop for the first time, she had been genuinely happy for her. But then there was that twinge of something as Captain Braddock told Sally the story of the *Anne* and the first Captain Jeremiah's nearly disastrous encounter with pirates. And in the kitchen just now, as the three finished up the dishes and said goodnight, Sally had said something that made Mrs. James laugh so hard, and Katherine had felt—yes, there it was.

She drew in a deep breath and shut her eyes again, determined to face it in all its ugliness. It *was* jealousy, or maybe at its simplest, fear... the fear of being left out or left behind somehow, the fear of change.

Lord, she prayed as hurt and shame and humiliation swept over her, *I know this isn't right. It isn't rational, but it's there and real and...and it hurts. Forgive me for being jealous, and for being afraid. I know in my head that no one wants to leave me out. Help me to feel it in my heart as well.*

A tear trickled down Katherine's cheek, then another, as she leaned her head on the windowpane and, as Mrs. James often advised her to, she "told God all about it."

9

No Fear in Love

Katherine drifted awake to the sound of driving rain against the window. She had fallen asleep in the window seat, with her head against the glass. Sitting up and stretching, she tried to ease the stiffness from her limbs. From the faint kitchen sounds rising through the heating vent, she knew that Mrs. James—and likely Sally, too—must be downstairs doing the morning baking.

She could go down and help, but it was Saturday, her day off. She considered crawling into her bed and going back to sleep, but decided to get dressed and make the most of being already awake.

Standing stiffly, she took the corner of a blanket and rubbed at the faint smudge her forehead had made where she leaned against the glass. She made a mental note to find some glass cleaner downstairs later, then looked beyond the glass at the dark, heavy clouds, barely visible through the pouring rain. A deep sigh welled up inside her. October had arrived.

* * * *

A half-hour later, Katherine descended the stairs in a long skirt and her coziest sweater, wet curls pulled into a messy bun. She found Mrs. James and Sally in the kitchen.

"Good morning, Dearie. Glad you came down." Mrs. James wiped her hands on her apron before giving Katherine a quick one-armed squeeze. "I'm covered with flour this morning, else I'd give you a proper hug. Any nice plans for your day off?"

"Not exactly. I had thought of going on a walk, but this rain..."

Mrs. James nodded, glancing out the small window over the sink. "It sure is wet out there today." She eyed Katherine for a moment. "Tea and a book, then?"

Katherine grinned. "You know me so well! Yes, I was hoping for a pot of tea to take upstairs."

"I already have one brewing for you. And Sally's just about to pull a batch of her scones from the oven, so you can take a plate of those with you, if you like."

"That would be perfect!" Turning to Sally, Katherine asked, "You made the scones yourself?"

Sally smiled nervously. "Yes. Aunt Harriet has been teaching me. My first batch wasn't very good, though."

"Neither was mine. I forgot a step, and they turned out almost inedible. I did get the hang of it after a while, though."

"I hope I will. The dough did *seem* all right this morning, but you never know what might happen in there." Sally eyed the large oven warily.

"I'm sure they'll be delicious." Katherine turned towards Mrs. James. "Is there anything I can do to help while I'm waiting for the scones to come out?"

"Not a thing. In fact, your tea's just about ready. Let me pop a cozy over the pot, and you can take it on up. And I'll bring your scones up to you when they come out."

"Sure." Katherine said brightly, trying to hide a little prick of disappointment. She had hoped for a few minutes to talk things over with Mrs. James, but she could see that this wouldn't be a good time. She put on a smile. "Thank you. I can come back down for the scones if you like. It doesn't seem fair to make you come all the way up just to bring me food."

"Nonsense." Mrs. James said, giving her shoulders another quick squeeze. "It's your day off, and since you're stuck indoors, you'll just have to let me pamper you a bit."

Katherine wrapped her friend in a hug, flour and all, then took the tray and started up the stairs to her room. It was nice to be appreciated, but the nagging hurt hadn't gone away overnight. Leaving the door ajar, she set the tray down on a little table near the window seat and poured herself a cup. A smile spread over her face as she recognized the aroma of her favorite blend.

Sally's tirade at Rosie had held one true thing: Mrs. James was indeed the kindest woman she'd ever met, and so thoughtful. Looking down at her teacup, Katherine had no doubt she was loved. She let out a long breath. *So why do I still feel afraid?*

* * * *

Katherine sat curled up in a blanket on the window seat, Bible in her lap and fingers wrapped around a warm cup of tea when a soft knock on the door made her look up.

"I've brought your scones," Mrs. James said gently, stepping in and closing the door behind her. "And I can tell you've something weighing on you. Do you need to talk?"

Katherine hesitated, "But the shop...the first of the dailies will be in soon."

"I told Sally to come up and fetch me if it gets too much for her. She really has improved the past few days, and a little responsibility won't hurt. Besides, there won't be many brave enough to venture out in all this rain." Mrs. James moved a pillow off the other end of the window seat and asked, "May I?"

"Of course." Katherine smiled, curling her feet closer to make room

"Now, this thing that's weighing you down, does it need talking out, or is it something you just need to take to the Lord?"

"I don't know." Katherine said, frowning. "Part of me feels like I should be able to figure this out myself, but I honestly don't know how."

Mrs. James gestured to the open Bible on Katherine's lap. "Well, it looks like you've got a good start anyway."

"I'm trying." Katherine ran her thumb absent-mindedly over the corner of the pages.

"Would this have anything to do with Sally being here, and things being different?"

Katherine's eyes widened. "How did you know?"

"Just a little educated guess, Dearie."

Katherine drew in a long breath. "It's just... for so long I didn't really have anyone. I mean, I had my parents, but I'd pushed them out of my heart."

Mrs. James nodded, a look of sympathetic understanding in her eyes.

"I've been so enjoying being loved by the people I love, but now there's this fear, that... I don't even know exactly what I'm afraid of, but I am."

Mrs. James sat still for a moment, gazing out at the driving rain. Then without turning, she said sofly, *"There is no fear in love; but perfect love casteth out fear: because fear hath torment. He that feareth is not made perfect in love."* She smiled at Katherine and gently took the Bible from her lap.

Placing the ribbon marker where Katherine had been reading, Mrs. James flipped the pages quickly. She handed it back, and put her finger on the page. "Here, 1 John 4:18. It's a verse I've had to cling to much over the past two years."

Katherine looked up, eyes wide with surprise. "You have?"

"Yes. You see, Katherine, God designed us to love as He loves, but human love falls short every time. We so often base our love solely on emotions, and fixate on how we feel. But feelings are fleeting, so this kind of feeling-based love creates fear, and that fear torments us. The more we fear, the more selfish and self-centered we become, and that in turn intensifies our fear, and so it goes, on and on."

"So, what's the answer?"

Mrs. James reached over and gently tapped the page. "This. You need to get to know *God's* love so that you can tell true from false. Then, when you are tempted to fear or jealousy or envy, you can recognize that love doesn't envy, it isn't jealous or self-seeking. It doesn't doubt or fear, but believes and hopes."

"That's from 1 Corinthians, isn't it?" Katherine kept her place with one finger while flipping back the pages.

"Yes, chapter 13."

A faint clatter sounded from downstairs, and Mrs. James stood reluctantly to her feet. "I suppose I should go check how Sally's getting on." Squeezing Katherine's hand, she said softly, "Don't forget to eat your scones while they're warm, Dearie."

Katherine returned the squeeze, eyes shining with tears. As her motherly friend gently pulled the door shut, Katherine settled further into her nest of blankets and pillows and began to read about God's love, and to talk to Him about how her own love had fallen short.

* * * *

"Why, Katherine, I didn't expect a visit on yer day off." Captain Braddock said as Katherine came through the door of the Harborside later that day. He helped her with her jacket, hanging it on the coatrack and saying with a wink, "Of course, I can't say I'm at all displeased."

Katherine smiled, and again felt how wrong she had been to be jealous the day before.

"I thought today might be a good day to look through some of the sea chests in the tower, like you had talked about the other day."

"Ah, yes. It's just the day for it. I'll fetch the key from my desk and we'll go up." He stopped to check the thermometer and adjust the door of the wood stove on the way to his desk. "Mind bringing an empty box from the storeroom in case we want to bring anything down to sort where it's warm?"

Katherine's hand was on the door handle by the time he had finished his sentence. "Of course! I'll be right back."

The storeroom was dark and cold, the air filled with an odd combination of mustiness and fragrance. It had been used to house shipments of tea ever since the Harborside was expanded by an enterprising Braddock in the Victorian era.

In the old days, the tea business had occupied the whole block-long brick building, but over the years business had declined to the point that the family was forced to sell all but the three small rooms on one end. In more recent days, the decline had become so severe that the shop was almost lost altogether.

Katherine shuddered as she remembered how much Captain Braddock had been willing to give up in order to save the place. She was so thankful they had found a way to save both the shop and Captain Braddock's retirement savings.

Katherine scanned the dark corners of the room. She had never seen the storeroom even close to full. She sighed and walked down the stairs. *One day,* she thought, *perhaps the Harborside will need all this space, and even be able to gain back the rest of the building.*

She shook her head at her own optimism. Even with the recent upturn in sales, that seemed too much to dream. She grabbed an empty box from a pile near the door and headed back up the stairs.

A thrill of excitement ran through her as she neared the spiral staircase. The room at the top had been kept a secret for so long, Katherine never lost the feeling of entering a hidden world when she walked through the doorway at the top of the stairs.

Today it seemed otherworldly, indeed, with a pale blue light flooding the space, dimly contrasting with the cozy glow of lamps in the shop below. She stood a moment on the threshold, the box dangling from one hand, gazing with anticipation at the sea trunks, resting securely beneath the rain-pelted windows.

The trunks had beckoned to her ever since that first day when Captain Braddock took her into the secret tower. Now, she surveyed them one by one, wondering which they would get to open today. Although the trunks were of similar shape and size, each one was unique in some way.

Katherine heard the captain's footsteps on the stairs behind her and turned, saying, "Which trunk did you want to look through first?"

"I thought we'd look through this one." He nodded towards the rectangular chest closest to the door. He stiffly maneuvered himself down onto his knees next to the trunk and reached for the lid. Katherine knelt beside him, eager-eyed and breathless with the thrill of new discovery.

The metal hinges gave a soft squeak as the lid was raised, and a faint smell of cedar wafted up from inside. A shuffled mass of papers filled the shallow tray on top, and Captain Braddock shook his head at the sight of them.

"I'm afraid these are all in quite a mess. Grandma Braddock was a wonderful woman, and loved this place dearly, but organization wasn't her greatest quality. She had a habit of keeping the mundane all mixed together with the important. It's left to us to sort out which is which." He looked over at Katherine and asked, "You up for the job?"

Katherine grinned. "Of course!"

Captain Braddock struggled to his feet, leaning heavily on the edge of the trunk. "We could bring the whole tray down, but why don't you grab a couple handfuls and we'll look through them downstairs by the stove—just in case a customer comes in." He winked and started down the stairs.

Katherine began gently gathering up some of the papers. She loved things like this, picking over little bits of history. That was why she had chosen to major in history at college. And with the way the Braddocks held on to tradition and family history, there was a good chance of finding something truly significant in amongst the ordinary details of life as a tea seller.

* * * *

"Receipt...receipt...grocery list..." Captain Braddock tossed several papers into the wooden crate which held kindling for the wood stove, and then opened the stove door to add another log. The flames licked over the new piece of wood and for a few moments the only sounds in the shop were the cozy crackling of flames and the rustling of papers.

"Recipe for beef stew..."

"I'll take that one. I have a little pile of recipes over here."

"Here you are, then." He held the paper out to her without lifting his eyes. "Receipt...receipt...Ah, here's our first treasure!" The captain's eyes twinkled as he held out a faded photograph.

Katherine reached over to take the picture gingerly by its edges. A gangly boy and a petite girl stood side by side, dressed in the simple attire of pioneer children. "Is this you and Serena?"

Captain Braddock chuckled. "Yes, though you wouldn't think it, the way I look now."

"What were you dressed up for?"

"Harborhaven used to have a festival every year. I can't think what they called it... But they had all the descendants of the founding families march in a parade down main street, and then down to the wharf, where they would have all manner of wooden ships moored. Sometimes, there was even a boat race!" He chuckled again and shook his head. "Those were the days."

"I remember seeing pictures from something like that at the historical society's museum. I wonder why they don't have that festival anymore?"

"I don't know. They stopped while I was away at sea. I should ask Serena."

His words trailed off and both lapsed into a thoughtful silence. Katherine sat looking at the picture, an idea taking shape in her heart and mind. Captain Braddock looked over and raised one eyebrow in mock concern.

"Uh-oh. I know that look. What are you plotting, then, Missy?"

Katherine shook her head. "Not plotting, only dreaming."

"And what are you dreaming about?"

"I'm not quite sure yet." Katherine felt that the seed of

an idea had been planted, but couldn't yet tell what it would become.

* * * *

The wind and rain continued throughout the day and into the evening. Katherine had lingered near the Harborside's warm stove as long as possible before starting off for Miss Harriet's.

As she neared the last block, she slowed her pace, pulled her jacket close around her, and began silently to pray. *Lord, there is no fear in Your love. Help me not to fear, but to trust. Help me not to be jealous. Help me to love as You love, and not to focus on myself.*

As she neared the tea room, Katherine could see light spilling through the lace curtains and making bright pools on the sidewalk in the stormy darkness. Glancing in, she could see the two ladies clearing tables, chatting and laughing as they worked. The all-too-familiar pang pricked her heart, and she took a deep breath before opening the door. "*There is no fear in love, for perfect love casteth out fear.*"

10

The Anne

"Hi there, Tommy." Katherine tossed her hat onto the coatrack and unbuttoned her jacket. "I see the captain's got you hard at work."

"Uh-huh." Tommy replied without looking up.

Katherine couldn't help but smile at the earnestness of the small boy's face as he sat on the floor dusting a jar from the lowest shelf.

"Tommy." The firmness in Captain Braddock's tone was unmistakable, even from the other room. "How do we answer grownups in the shop?"

"Oh, right." Tommy turned his little face upwards to look Katherine in the eyes. "Yes, Ma'am."

Captain Braddock appeared in the doorway to the Captain's Quarters, eyes twinkling. "That's the way. Well done, my boy. Hello, Katherine."

"Hello. I've brought Miss Harriet's order." She handed the

slip of paper to the captain. "Is there anything I can help with while I'm here?"

"You might help Tommy with the top rows of shelves. He can't quite reach those yet."

"But the captain says I'm gonna grow soon!" Tommy said, looking up again, his face alight with anticipation.

"Yes you are, my boy, but until then, you're going to leave the top ones to the big folk, and not go climbin' the shelves again, right?"

Tommy nodded solemnly. "Right."

"*Again?*" Katherine raised her eyebrows as she looked from Tommy to the captain.

"Let's just say we're both still learning about little boys in tea shops—even though I was one once, and ought to know all about it."

Tommy's head shot up in surprise. "Captain, *you* were a boy once? Here? Like me?"

Katherine wondered if his eyes could possibly open any wider.

"Yes, Tommy, I was the Harborside's little boy once, just like you are now." He limped over to the staircase and lowered himself onto a step. "And what's more, I sat in that very spot dusting those very same jars."

Katherine looked over at the boy and discovered that Tommy's eyes actually *could* get wider.

"The same jars?" he asked, voice hushed with wonder. He looked down at his hands, then held up the rag. "With this?"

The old man chuckled and reached out to muss the boy's hair. "No, my rags wore out and had to be replaced. But the jars are the same, and some of the dust, too, no doubt." He winked at Katherine, who had fetched two rags and joined them by the shelves.

Lifting the *Anne* from an upper shelf, she reverently handed the model ship to the captain, along with a rag. He smiled and nodded, and Katherine enjoyed the moment of mutual understanding. With another glance at the boy, he began the careful, painstaking process of giving the ship a full "swabbing," as they called it.

Katherine picked up a jar and started dusting. She sensed a story coming, and her heart quickened its pace in anticipation.

"Well, now" Captain Braddock began, eyes still focused on the minutia of the rigging as he cleaned off the dust. "Have I ever told either of you about how the very first Captain Braddock came to own the *Anne?*"

They both shook their heads, and a thrill ran through Katherine. Lifting a tea bowl off the shelf, she turned to watch the captain as she slowly wiped it clean.

"Well, it all started when Jeremiah Braddock and his young wife Anne came over from England. He wasn't a captain then, you see, just the son of a shipwright, looking for a fresh start in the shipyards of New England.

"It was a lengthy voyage, and Jeremiah spent his days up on deck, talking to the crew. He'd grown up building ships, you see, but never had a chance to sail aboard one. By the time land was in sight, Jeremiah had talked the crew into letting him help with the different jobs aboard ship.

"Between his knowledge of the ship's construction and the hours he'd spent watching, listening, and working alongside the sailors, he'd built up a considerable understanding of both ship and crew.

"When they arrived in America, he began looking for work. He started off doing what he knew, working for a large shipyard in Baltimore, but he never forgot those days aboard ship. His wife always said she could tell then he'd been smitten with life aboard ship, and admitted she used to pray every night when they first arrived that he'd not leave her alone in the strange new land and go off to sea."

Captain Braddock tipped the *Anne* carefully and worked his rag around the tiny deck fittings. Tommy scooted close and inspected the ship as the captain continued.

"He was a quick one, Jeremiah was, and soaked up learning like a sponge. Whenever he had opportunity, he talked to the wealthy merchants who came to see the progress he was making on their ships, and as he rose from one position to another, he soon began to build friendships with the merchants.

"One day, he heard a couple of the merchants talking about a new ship, the *Rainbow*, that had made the trip to China in record time. It intrigued Jeremiah, and he asked the men all sorts of questions about the ship's design. The owner of the shipyard found Jeremiah later on and told him one of the men had commissioned the yard to build a ship faster than the *Rainbow*, and that the man also told him he wanted Jeremiah to design it.

"Jeremiah was dumbfounded. He'd designed a few of the smaller sailing ships on his own, and drawn up plans for several big vessels, but he had never been able to build any of his larger designs. However, since hearing about the *Rainbow*'s slim hull and large sail area, he'd already begun designing a similar ship in his mind.

"He told the owner that he would take on the job, but only if the shipyard would increase his pay. He and Anne had a little one on the way by then, you see.

"The owner agreed, and Jeremiah got to work. Anne used to tell her children of the long hours Jeremiah spent at the kitchen table late into the night, candle burning, pencil in hand, working away at the plans for the ship that was to be faster than the *Rainbow*.

"One day, when the ship was nearly finished, Jeremiah got called into the head man's office again. He told Jeremiah that he had bad news, that the man who commissioned the ship had pulled out of the deal, went bankrupt, in fact, and left them high and dry with a ship they probably couldn't sell, the design being new and untested.

"Jeremiah, though shocked at the news, sat a moment then asked, 'Sir, what if I could bring this company the same amount of money the man would have paid you for the ship. Would you let me have her?' The man was speechless, and just sorta stared at him for a while. Finally, he asked what Jeremiah had in mind.

"'A voyage.' Jeremiah said. 'I'll take her on a merchant run and bring back more than enough cargo to pay for the ship.' The man sat back in his chair and studied Jeremiah's face. 'You'll need a captain and crew.'

"Jeremiah's heart lifted at that. 'I'll find a crew,' he said, 'and train them how to sail her, as that other man had asked me to do. If I can't find a good captain for her, I'll command her myself.' Seeing the man's face grow doubtful, he said, 'and if I don't recoup yer losses, you can fire me on the spot.'

"And so Jeremiah set off on his first true adventure at sea. He christened the ship the *Anne*, after his wife, and somehow managed to find a crew. He commanded the ship himself, but hired an experienced sailor as his first mate, a friend of his whom he could trust. And then—"

All three jumped at the ring of the bell over the shop door.

"Tommy, time to go." A tall woman with a rather passive face appeared in the doorway, hand still on the antique doorhandle as she stood, obviously in a hurry.

"Aw...Cap'n was just about to tell me the rest of the story. Can't I stay?" Tommy's tone was high and whiny, and Katherine noticed Captain Braddock frown.

"Now, young man. That's no way to speak to yer mother. She's let you stay this long, for which we should be grateful." He gently nudged the boy to his feet. "I'll tell you the rest tomorrow, never fear."

Tommy looked up into the Captain's face, torn between anticipation and petulance. "Yes, Sir, Cap'n." Then with a half smile at Katherine, he said, "See you tomorrow." And with a hurried thanks directed toward the captain, Tommy's mother propelled him through the doorway and shut the door firmly behind her.

Katherine picked up the rag and jar Tommy had left on the floor. "You know, I've never heard that story either. Will you tell me the rest of it?"

A twinkle appeared in Captain Braddock's eyes. "But then Tommy would be disappointed I told it without him. You'll just have to wait, Missy." He winked, and Katherine couldn't help but chuckle.

"I think I'll have just as hard a time waiting as Tommy will."

"Ah, but it'll be worth it, now, won't it?"

She gave a mock frown. "It had better be."

* * * *

It was a chilly night as Katherine walked home. She walked down the wharf that stretched along the harbor through the length of what used to be the downtown merchant blocks.

Looking up into the crisp black of the clear sky, with countless stars shimmering softly, she prayed, *Lord, You made all those stars, and placed them each where they should be.*

A warm joy welled up inside her as she stopped to gaze up at the sky, elbows propped on the rough wood of the weather-beaten railing.

And You placed me just where I should be, too. Thank You, Lord. Thank You for bringing me out of my bitterness and pain. Thank You for giving me the Harborside and Miss Harriet's. Thank You for the captain and Mrs. James. Oh, and thank you for Tommy. I haven't seen the captain so happy since Serena's visit. Thank You for giving him a new purpose and someone so precious to invest in.

She reluctantly pushed herself off the railing and began walking again. Sally's face came before her mind's eye.

Lord, I don't know how to help her. I want to, but...I just don't know how. Please open the door a little further. And help my jealousy and fears not to ruin any opportunities to share Your truth with her.

With a deep sigh, she looked up. She was just passing the end of the brick block that used to belong to the Harborside.

And Lord, is it even possible that the captain could gain back the Harborside's whole building one day?

11

Forgiven

Sunday dawned with unexpected blue skies and morning sunlight warmer than Katherine would have thought possible for mid-October. After rummaging through her church clothes, she put on her favorite navy dress, layering a soft cardigan with the luxurious silvery scarf Mrs. James had given her for Christmas her first year back in Harborhaven.

After arranging the scarf, she surveyed the results in the long mirror next to the coatrack by the door. She loved how graceful the long dress made her feel, and couldn't resist a twirl as she reached for her jacket and purse. She knew how childish she must have appeared, but looking down at the soft, flowing hem that swung just above her church shoes, she decided that there were some things she would never outgrow.

She checked her watch as she came down the stairs and into the soft gold light which bathed the tearoom. *Ten minutes.*

She crossed the room and ducked into the kitchen to put the kettle on, then looked in the refrigerator to see what leftovers remained from the day before. With a triumphant smile, she took out a tray of pasties and set it on the counter. Hopping up onto a small step they kept stashed in one corner of the kitchen, she reached for the picnic basket on top of the cupboards.

By the time the big kettle began to sing, she had the pasties wrapped in wax paper and stowed away in the basket, along with two apples, some of Sally's scones, and a couple tiny jars of cream and jam. She found room in the refrigerator for the basket and turned her attention to the teapot.

* * * *

Katherine had just finished pouring out the tea when she heard Mrs. James unlock and open the front door. With a smile of satisfaction, she fit the lids on four "to-go" cups. *Four.* Sally had agreed to come to church with them that morning, and Katherine's heart fluttered with hopeful expectation.

"About ready, Dearie?" Mrs. James peeked at her around the kitchen curtain.

"Yes, I'm ready. Could you take a couple of these?" Katherine held out two cups, fragrant steam curling up from the travel lids.

"What a wonderful idea!" Mrs. James reached for the cups and held the curtain back with her arm. Katherine took the remaining two cups of tea and they walked out to where Mr. James was waiting in his car.

"What's this?" he asked as his wife handed him a cup.

"Tea for the road, compliments of Katherine."

Mr. James' face grew serious, but his eyes twinkled at Katherine in the rear-view mirror as she slid into the back seat. "Ah, but is it Assam?"

"Not today," Katherine said, quickly adding, "This is the new Cameroonian tea. I thought you would all like to try it."

"Well, I suppose it's good to try new things from time to time." Mr. James tried to pull his face into a serious expression, but the corners of his mouth gave a telling twitch.

"It does smell delicious!" Mrs. James said, lifting the cup closer to her face and breathing deeply.

"I agree," Mr. James said, back to his usual cheery tone. He turned the car around and headed down Main Street.

The Victorian brick buildings of the downtown blocks slid swiftly past the windows as Katherine held two cups on her lap. She couldn't decide if the strange, tingly feeling in her stomach was nervousness or anticipation. Perhaps it was both. *Please, Lord, help Sally.*

They stopped outside one of the taller buildings and waited. The shops on the main level were dark and still, but a familiar form emerged from the sheltered doorway, black skirt and white blouse mostly hidden under a warm jacket.

"Good morning, Sally!" Katherine said as the younger woman plopped onto the seat next to her.

"Mornin'," she mumbled, settling down into her seat with a posture that reminded Katherine of a turtle retreating into its shell.

"Tea," Katherine said gently, holding out the cup.

"Thank you." A faint glimmer of a smile flickered across

Sally's face before she turned back toward the window, both hands curled tightly around her cup of tea.

* * * *

The ride to church was subdued, but cheerful. Katherine was surprised that Sally could keep up her solemn silence when the sun shone so gloriously through the yellow-orange leaves that still clung to the branches of trees along the road. But then, Katherine remembered how even the beauty of her beloved harbor had failed to cheer her during those first few months after her return to Harborhaven.

Katherine reached over and touched Sally's arm. "It's such a nice day, I wondered if you would want to come for a picnic after church?"

Sally's eyes lit up just a little and she nodded shyly. "I'd like that."

"What a great idea, Katherine. I hope there were some good leftovers for you to take."

"Oh, yes. There were pasties and some of Sally's delicious scones."

Another almost-smile from Sally. *Small victories.* Katherine thought.

* * * *

A dry carpet of leaves crunched under foot that afternoon as they neared the top of the long flight of stairs that connected downtown Harborhaven with the cliffs above. Out of breath, the two young women stopped to rest.

"Well, we made it." Katherine grinned.

"We did. Thanks for insisting on carrying the hamper. If not, I'd have quit halfway." Sally leaned back against the railing next to the stairs, making no effort to mask her heavy breathing.

Katherine set the large basket down and shifted the strap of her knapsack. "I come here often on my day off. Turn around and you'll see why."

Sally turned around and Katherine heard a sharp gasp that she knew had nothing to do with the long, steep flight of stairs they had just climbed.

The Victorian buildings of downtown Harborhaven parted at First street, drawing the eye down its length to the sparkling blue of the harbor, reflecting the bright blue of the sky overhead. Puffy clouds floated here and there above the horizon, completing the picture.

Sally stood, silent and speechless, and Katherine did, too. She let the beauty of the scene wash over her, undiminished by its familiarity. Katherine let her mind drift back to previous fall days, full of light and laughter and the feeling of being safe, secure with her parents. Glancing over at Sally, she wondered if her friend had ever experienced those things for herself.

Finally, Sally broke the silence. "And you grew up *here*?" Her eyes were still on the waters of the harbor, where the light breeze made tiny ripples across its surface, bouncing the sunlight off in sparks and glimmers.

"Yes. I did."

"And was it always...like this?"

"No. but it was always beautiful. My house faced the

harbor, and my room was right at the top, with a window that peeked over the trees and housetops. The harbor was usually the first thing I saw each morning."

Sally turned towards Katherine, a spark of interest in her face. "And when you left?"

Katherine gave a wry smile. "My window looked out on a grimy brick wall."

"Oh." Sally's voice came out in a whisper.

Katherine took a deep breath and said, "Well, I'm rested up now. Want to find a place to eat our picnic?"

Sally nodded and they walked on, but Katherine sensed a new bond of understanding between them.

* * * *

Katherine pulled a light blanket out of her knapsack and flung it out under the outspread arms of a large tree. They settled down onto the bumpy ground and started to unpack the basket. Sally suddenly giggled.

Katherine shot an amused glance her way. "What's so funny?"

"Didn't you just hear my stomach rumble? It was so loud! I didn't realize I was *that* hungry."

"We'd better finish getting this food out, then." Katherine chuckled. "Mind if I pray?"

Sally nodded and grinned. "I don't *think* I'll starve before you're through...if you're quick about it."

Katherine quickly thanked God for their food, and for Sally, adding a silent prayer for her friend, and for wisdom to know how to help.

They ate and chatted, and Katherine enjoyed her friend's new measure of openness. Finally, she felt confident enough to ask the question that had been burning in her all afternoon. Knowing a casual tone would be neither convincing nor honest, Katherine looked her friend straight in the eyes and just let the question flow out. "What did you think about church this morning?"

She sensed a wall go up as Sally's face clouded.

"I don't know...I didn't really understand much." She looked at Katherine and then took a breath. "Some of it sounded familiar, like how you and Auntie H. always talk. I suppose..."

Sally's voice trailed off and she looked down at the blanket. She picked crumbs up off the blanket, her face still clouded and a faraway look in her eyes. Suddenly looking up, she met Katherine's gaze with an intensity Katherine had never seen before.

"Doesn't it ever scare you?"

"What do you mean?" Katherine kept her voice even and calm, while inwardly pleading for wisdom.

"I mean, God. Doesn't God ever scare you? If He's perfect like the minister said..."

"Ah." Katherine nodded, considering. "Yes, the idea of a perfectly good God who judges sin can be a terrifying thought. But His forgiveness changes that. God *is* good, but He is also loving, and the Bible says that His perfect love casts out all fear."

Sally looked down again and mumbled. "But there are some things beyond forgiveness."

Katherine's heart swelled with sympathy for her friend.

Reaching over, she put her hand on Sally's shoulder and said softly. "*Nothing* is beyond His forgiveness."

"But you don't *know...*" Sally lifted red-rimmed eyes to Katherine's, filled with tears ready to overflow.

Katherine kept her gaze steady. "Do you want to tell me?" A long silence passed between them. Finally, Sally nodded.

"Can we walk?" she asked. "I think it would be easier if... if I didn't have to look at you while I said it."

Katherine nodded and began packing things back into the basket. When they had gathered everything, Katherine hunched the knapsack onto her back and reached for the hamper.

"I'll take that this time," Sally said, grasping the handle.

The two walked along the path to where one branch of it wound off along the top of the cliffs overlooking the harbor. Katherine led them down the winding path and they walked in silence for a while. As Katherine kept pace with her friend, her heart raced, a churning mass of concern, sympathy, awareness of her own inadequacy, and yes, even a faint sense of hope.

Finally, as they turned down a more secluded part of the trail, Sally spoke up.

"It was my brother." Her voice was full of sorrow, but with an edge of hardness to it. "He and I were always close, especially when Mum died. I was only eight, and he eleven. Well, Dad remarried, and although we missed Mum terribly, we promised him that we would try to love the new woman. We couldn't call her Mum, though, and she didn't want that either. We called her Mother. It was stiff and cold and distant —which in the end, fitted her perfectly.

"We did like her at first, but then the baby came, and all her love and attention went to her own child. Then there was another, and another. Eventually there was quite a large family of her own children, and she took to sending the two of us away to anyone who would take us, to get us 'out from under foot' as she called it. She pretended it was meant to be a treat for us, but to my brother and me, it was plain as plain she wanted rid of us so she could have just her *own* family together.

"We lived far from Gran, and Mother wouldn't let us visit much. I think Gran would have tried to take us in for good, if she'd known how things really were. But for all our hurt, we were afraid to tell anyone how bad things had gotten."

They stepped to one side to let a jogger pass, then Sally continued.

"Finally, my brother couldn't stand it anymore. He said he would run away and join the Guards or the Navy. But they wouldn't take him. Something about his heart. He left anyway, and Mother wouldn't let him see me anymore. She made sure there was always one of her children with me when I went anywhere so I couldn't sneak away to meet him.

"One night, I did sneak away. I found where he'd said he was living—a horrible place, dark and cold, and it stank. He told me there was a way out. He said he was going to London, and begged me to come with him. I wanted to, but I was afraid. By then, the woman we called Mother had become so angry at us, I often had to wear long sleeves, even in summer, to hide the bruises."

Katherine's stomach tightened. How much Sally had suffered!

"I was a coward." Sally's voice broke as she choked back a sob. "I went back to gather my things, but she found me packing and I was so scared, I—*I told her.*" Sally covered her face with her hands, her body stiff and taut, as if braced against a sudden jolt. Katherine put her arm around the rigid shoulders but stayed silent, sensing there was more.

Wiping her hand across her eyes, Sally lifted her head and continued. "I don't know why she wanted to keep my brother from going to London, but she locked me in my room and I heard her on the phone with the police, making up some story about him to get them to find him for her. She acted the part of the concerned mother, but I knew the truth.

"Somehow, he got out of town before the police could find him, but on the way to London—" Sally stood still and looked up at the sky, squeezing her eyes shut to keep back the tears. An anguished whisper finally squeaked out from between her lips. "He was on a motorcycle, and there was a crash."

Katherine drew her friend into her arms. "He didn't survive?" She felt her friend shake her head, and then the dam burst. Tears streamed down Sally's face and sobs racked her body. Sally stood, fists clenched, body stiff. Katherine held her friend, unsure what else to do. She had never experienced such deep agony, such guilt and anger. How could she help her friend see the truth?

"Sally," she said softly as her friend's sobs subsided and she pulled away to wipe her face with the edge of her sleeve. "Sally, will you look at me?"

Sally looked up, eyes full of uncertainty.

"*Nothing* is beyond God's forgiveness, if you ask for it."

"But I betrayed him. *My own brother!*"

Katherine stood silent for a moment, then began softly. "Remember how I told you that Jesus died to pay for our sins?"

"Yes."

"Well, while Jesus was on trial, being lied about by false witnesses and sentenced to that painful death, a man named Peter stood outside. He was Jesus' friend, maybe even like a brother. Three times, people asked if he was with Jesus, and three times, he denied even knowing Him.

"Instead of standing up for his Friend, Peter denied Him. He had said he was with Jesus to the death, but when the time came, he was afraid, and lied to protect himself. And Sally—Jesus forgave him." She looked directly into Sally's eyes. "*Nothing* is beyond His forgiveness. Not even a betrayal."

Sally sniffed and stuffed her hands in her pockets. "Can we keep walking?" she asked, eyes on her shoes.

"Sure." They walked together in silence a while longer. Katherine couldn't decide whether Sally could handle more, but she sensed she needed to hear it. "Can I tell you something else?" she asked gently.

Sally gave her a quick glance, then nodded.

"Your brother..." Katherine stopped, unsure how to phrase what she wanted to say. *Lord, give me words!* "From what you just told me, you couldn't have stopped him from going. And you definitely couldn't have protected him from that accident."

Katherine stopped and turned her friend's shoulders to face her. She spoke slowly, and with certainty. "You didn't kill your brother."

Sally stopped abruptly, looking steadfastly at her feet. "But if he hadn't been hurrying to get away—"

"Would that have changed anything? Wasn't he planning to take you to London that night, even before you told your stepmother about it?"

Sally's face crumpled, and her fists clenched. "But I wasn't there. I didn't go with him. It should have been him and me on that bike together. Maybe if I'd gone—"

Katherine placed one hand gently on Sally's shoulder. "You can't know what would have happened. Sally, the only thing you can know for sure is what *did* happen. You didn't stay behind on purpose, you were locked in your room. There was nothing you could have done to stop it. It wasn't your fault he died."

Sally pulled her arms across her middle and whispered, "But I *lived*."

Katherine's heart sank. *There it is.* She thought, heart almost breaking for her friend. This was the real source of her friend's guilt and remorse.

"That wasn't your fault either." she said gently. "Has it ever occurred to you that there might be a reason you were kept from that accident?" Turning her friend toward her, she continued. "God has a purpose for you, Sally, a *good* and *loving* purpose. And nothing you have done or could ever do will change His love for you."

Suddenly, something seemed to break inside Sally. She turned and threw her arms around Katherine's neck, clinging tight. She was sobbing again, but Katherine sensed no defiance this time, nothing held back. They stood that way for a long time while Sally sobbed out years of guilt and pain.

Finally, she stepped back, dragging an already sodden sleeve across her face. "I'm sorry," she said, her voice barely above a whisper.

"Sally, I'm glad to be here for you, and that's the truth."

Sally mustered a watery half-smile. "You've said lots of true things today. Thank you." Her voice fell to a whisper again, but no tears fell this time.

Katherine hoped the compassion she felt for her friend showed in her smile. "You're welcome. Do you want to walk further?"

Sally shook her head. "I think I'm ready to start back now. I suppose we won't have time to see your neighborhood now?"

Katherine glanced up at the sun. Their talk had taken a while, and they still had to walk quite a distance back to the park entrance. She looked back at her friend. "I think we need to get back, but we can always come again."

Sally looked skeptical. "Truly? You don't mind, now that you... *know*?"

"Not at all, Sally. Nothing you told me today changes anything. God loves you just the same as He always has, and so do I."

Sally looked at her, thoughtful, exhausted, but with a look of hope in her eyes. "You really believe that He could love me?"

Katherine gave her friend another hug. "With all my heart. He can, and *does*."

Sally hugged back, then broke away, a thoughtful look on her face.

As they neared the stairs down to First Street, Sally asked,

"How do I...do it? I mean, how do I ask for forgiveness, like you said."

"Your Aunt Harriet is fond of saying that prayer is just telling it all to God. Tell Him what you told me, but most importantly, tell Him about the ways you know you have sinned, and ask Him to forgive you, believing that His death on the cross paid for your sin."

"That's it?"

"That's it."

"I don't have to do anything or say special words?"

"No. Prayer is just a conversation with God. Talk to Him like you would to me."

Sally turned to look out at the harbor, now a dusky mass beyond the dark shapes of the buildings. A light flicked on here and there as the two stood in silence. Then, letting out a long breath, Sally turned to Katherine.

"It's done. I feel... different, like everything's gone quiet inside."

"Rest for your soul." Katherine said quietly, her vision blurring with tears of joy.

"And...forgiveness." Sally's eyes were soft and wide with wonder.

12

The Rest of the Story

A different Sally descended the stairs into downtown Harborside that day. Katherine noticed it as they stood at the corner, waiting to cross the street. There was a calm about her Katherine had never seen before.

It wasn't just in her eyes and expression, either. The stillness of Sally's hands and feet as she stood, the slight lift to her chin, and the shoulders squared as she stood just a little taller. A wave of joy bubbled up inside Katherine as she realized her friend wasn't hiding anymore.

They walked through the familiar downtown blocks, and as before, Sally didn't seem to even see them, but this time, it was eagerness, not preoccupation that Katherine sensed in her friend. They spoke little, until they neared the last block.

"D'you suppose she's there?"

Katherine shrugged. "I don't know. She never comes in Sundays. It's her one true day off." She gave her friend an encouraging smile. "But you never know. She has a habit of showing up right when we need her."

Sally's steps quickened as they neared the shop. The sun had set while they walked, but through the dusk, light spilled onto the sidewalk from the tea shop's windows. Suddenly, Sally froze, her brows crumpled into a worried frown.

"What's wrong?" Katherine asked, turning to peer at her friend through the dim light.

"Oh, Katherine... whatever do I say?"

"Whatever's in your heart to say," Katherine chuckled. "If you're at all like me, one look at her and the words will just come tumbling out all over each other."

Sally grinned. "She does that to you too, huh?" They laughed together, and then Sally stepped quickly to the door.

Katherine unlocked the door.

"Is that you, Dearies?" Mrs. James' voice called out from the kitchen.

Katherine and Sally exchanged a grin, then Sally quickly crossed to the kitchen doorway. She hesitated just outside.

"Oh, Auntie!"

Katherine saw Sally run the last few steps into the kitchen, and the soft muffled sobs and soothing tones which followed told Katherine that her friend was safely in the arms of her aunt.

* * * *

"Hello the shop!" Katherine called out with a laugh as the bell jingled merrily overhead and a gust of wind and rain followed them into the Harborside.

"Why, Katherine! I didn't expect you today." Captain Braddock stepped in from the office, Tommy following close behind him.

"I wanted to make sure I didn't miss the end of that story you promised to finish. And I've brought Sally with me." Katherine threw a casual arm around her friend's shoulders. "Are we in time?"

"Of course." Captain Braddock winked. "You didn't think I'd forget my promise to wait till you both were here, now did you?"

"Certainly not." Katherine said with a teasing grin. "I just didn't want you to be tempted."

"Well then," Captain Braddock eased himself into the chair by the woodstove and reached for the poker. "Have a seat, if you ladies don't mind the floor. Better yet, Tommy, bring in my desk chair for our new friend, Miss Sally."

Sally plopped down on the floor, curling her legs and tucking the hem of her skirt under her. "I'm fine here."

Katherine sat beside her. "Me too."

"All we're missing is a cup of tea." Captain Braddock said with a wistful look toward the kitchen.

"I'll put the kettle on," said Tommy, halfway to the small hidden kitchen.

"Whoa, there, mister." Captain Braddock called out, his voice stern. "No mannin' the kitchen without a grownup."

"Can I help him?" asked Sally, scrambling to her feet.

Captain Braddock gave Katherine a questioning glance, and Katherine smiled and nodded.

"Thank you, Sally. Tommy knows where everything is, but don't let him climb on anything."

Sally nodded "Yes, sir."

Katherine scooted closer to Captain Braddock's chair and watched as he tended the fire. She loved the Harborside on these dark, cozy days when the biting cold and driving rain kept all but the most dedicated customers away. This was the season for spinning yarns in front of a fire, of just enjoying the company of her Harborside family—and now, Sally too. Somehow, she wanted Sally to experience the warmth and companionship for herself, to give her a glimpse of family as it should be.

Giggles and the soft thud of cupboard doors floated in through the office doorway, and Captain Braddock smiled. "Sounds like those two are getting along just fine."

Katherine nodded and stared at the flickering flames, leaning her head on the arm of the overstuffed chair with a happy sigh. She wanted to tell Captain Braddock about her conversation with Sally the day before, but knew it was Sally's news, not her own. Instead, she would try to be patient, and she would soak in every moment of this peaceful, joyous afternoon.

They sat in companionable silence until the kettle sang in the other room. Captain Braddock suddenly leaned toward her, his bushy white eyebrows raised and drawn together into an almost comical look of uncertainty. "She does *know* how to make tea, doesn't she?"

Katherine laughed. "Of course. I taught her myself."

A look of relief crossed his face. "Good. I wouldn't want to get caught between polite appreciation and a poorly brewed cup of tea."

"Here we are!" Sally's voice rang out as she marched

triumphantly through the door with an old wooden tray loaded with cups, saucers, and a steaming pot of tea.

"You even found the tray. Well done, my boy!" Captain Braddock reached over to tussle the boy's hair. "Now, bring over that little footstep by the shelves and that'll be yer table."

Sally poured out the tea, and handed a cup to Katherine and the Captain, then held one out to Tommy, who sat cross-legged behind the small wooden step. Captain Braddock took the cup from Sally's hand and placed it in front of the boy. "There y'are, young fella. Now try not to joggle the step or drop the cup, and you'll be just fine."

Tommy nodded, and stared down at his cup, fascinated by the steam rising off the surface of the deep golden liquid.

"What kind of tea is this? The leaves looked funny when I measured it out." Sally asked, blowing across the top of her sturdy white teacup.

"Gunpowder Green." Captain Braddock said, taking a sip. "And brewed just right. I see Katherine has taught you well."

Sally blushed, making no effort to hide the grin spreading over her face.

"The leaves of this particular tea are rolled up tight into little pellets. It's done by hand, which is quite time-consuming."

Tommy took a sip and wrinkled his nose. "It tastes fishy."

The captain's hearty laugh rang through the room. "At least you're honest, my boy. Go get the honeypot from off the counter and bring a small spoon from the drawer."

Tommy jumped up, only bumping the step a little in his haste.

As he disappeared into the kitchen, Katherine raised her eyebrows. "Honey?"

"I know. It isn't ideal. But young'uns need to be eased into it sometimes. That's how Great-grandma Braddock started Serena and me off. I had forgotten until Tommy came around."

"Here, Cap'n!" Tommy appeared with what appeared to Katherine a small urn with a wooden lid fitted into the top of it.

Katherine smiled at the boy's awestruck expression as he intently watched Captain Braddock twirl the wooden dipper to catch the golden glob of honey. She really couldn't blame him. There was something fascinating about the way the firelight from the wooden stove reflected off the fragrant honey, as if little bursts of flame had gotten stuck within the sticky liquid.

Sally raised her cup, and Katherine caught the faintest grimace cross her face as she tasted the tea. A glance at the captain told her he had noticed also.

"Here, hold yer cup out, there."

Sally did, and another luminous drop of honey was caught up and deposited, this time in Sally's cup. Sally smiled. "Thank you. It did taste a bit...I mean, I'm sure I'll learn to like it eventually."

"Gunpowder green is somewhat of an acquired taste. My sister Serena never quite learned to like it, and she ended up married to a Chinese tea planter!"

"Really?" Sally's eyes grew wide.

"Yes, indeed." Captain Braddock glanced over at Tommy, and said, "But that's a story for another day. I promised this young'n I'd finish telling about the first Captain Jeremiah Braddock and the maiden voyage of the *Anne*."

A flood of anticipation welled up inside Katherine, and she shifted her legs to a more comfortable position, settling in for what she knew would be a good story.

"So there he was, the first Captain Jeremiah Braddock, with ship and crew all ready to set sail. This was no ordinary ship, however. The *Anne* was modeled off the *Rainbow*, one of the earliest of the true clipper ships.

"Captain Jeremiah had no experience, of course, but he did have one major advantage with the crew. Since he designed the ship, he knew much more about the ship than they did. And it was no ordinary ship, either. The sailors soon found that he really did know what he was about.

"When the departure day arrived and the crew prepared to launch, Anne Braddock stood at the edge of the crowd, as near as she could safely go to her husband's ship. She waved farewell with one arm, holding their newborn son in the other.

"She was a mighty brave woman, Anne Braddock was. When the boy was born, Captain Jeremiah had offered to cancel the voyage altogether, but Anne was adamant that he should go. 'You've given your word, and that's that. I'll make do till you return. Just you come back to me, and I'll be content."

Captain Braddock glanced up at the thermometer on the wall and then reached over to open the door of the woodstove a little further.

"Well, he did go, and spent the first week of the voyage walking up and down the ship, talking to the sailors and helping them figure out the oddities of such a different sort of craft." He paused and nudged Tommy's shoulder. "Go get the *Anne* off her shelf, will ye? And mind yer teacup."

Tommy's tea splashed into the saucer as he hurried across the room to the shelves, stepping up on a small ladder to reach the top shelf.

"Ah, thank you, my boy." Taking the ship, Captain Braddock held it up for them to see. "The sails had to be carefully managed, see, because the hull was so sharp and shallow. Older ships had a rounder hull, but these clippers were streamlined to make them faster. That meant the ship rode differently in the waters than other ships, so the *Anne's* first voyage was a tricky thing."

"Where were they sailing to?" Sally asked, leaning forward, eyes sparkling with interest.

"To China, to pick up a cargo of tea. They would have sailed round the Cape of Good Hope, then up past Australia and the Philippines before heading into port. Foochow was the port they sailed the *Anne* into, I believe.

"Once into clear seas, the *Anne* made good time, and sailed into Foochow without incident. The journey back, however, was not so uneventful.

"They had docked at the Pagoda Anchorage in Foochow, which meant traversing the Min river. It was a narrow gorge with a fast current and high walls just barely passable for a ship with as much in the way of spars and rigging as the *Anne* had.

"At one point, a monkey got tangled with the tackle on one of the sails and had to be rescued. It was injured, so they took it below to be patched up, and the monkey became a sort of a pet. It stayed with them the rest of the voyage.

"Eventually, they made it through the tight gorge and out into open seas again. Two weeks into their journey, though, they ran into a typhoon. The ship nearly capsized in the fearsome winds. The sails hadn't been taken in properly, you see, and the ship was tipped to one side by the gusting wind.

"Captain Jeremiah used to tell his children that what scared him in that storm wasn't the steep angle of the deck, or the fierceness of the storm: it was the noises the ship made. All those timbers flexing and straining, groaning under its own weight at that unnatural angle.

"The crew hurried around, furling sails and doing everything the captain could think of to keep the ship from going over. He tried and tried, but nothing availed. He cried out to God, desperately asking for His mercy, while clinging to the ship with all his might.

"Suddenly, the storm moved off, and the ship righted. The sailors looked at each other, wide eyed, hearts beating, gasping for breath. They learned later on that another ship had been lost in that storm. Some said it was luck, some said it was just that the storm spent itself out, but Captain Jeremiah, *he* knew why the *Anne* had survived."

"Did God make the storm stop?" Tommy asked, head propped on his hands atop his makeshift table.

"I believe He did, Tommy, my boy."

Tommy's eyebrows scrunched together. "Does God always make the storms stop?"

"Not always, my boy. But He is so wise and so good and so

powerful, He knows just when a storm needs to be stopped, and when it needs to blow itself out."

Tommy laid his head on his arms and stared into the fire, deep in thought. After a moment, his head popped up again. "Did God stop storms when you were at sea?"

A faraway, awe-filled expression came into Captain Braddock's eyes as he looked down at the little boy. "Yes, He did at that. The very worst one I encountered, in fact." A car horn honked outside, and Captain Braddock sat back. "But that'll have to be a story for another day, because yer mother's here, and we musn't keep her waiting. Go and fetch yer jacket."

"Yes, Sir." Tommy's voice held a note of disappointment as he rose to his feet. Thrusting his arms into his jacket, he gave them a wave and a brief grin before tumbling out into the cold and wind between the shop and his mother's waiting car.

Katherine quietly rose and began gathering the tea things. As she walked into the little kitchen, she heard Captain Braddock's voice. "Now then, young Miss Sally. I see you've got a different sort of cheerfulness about you today. What might that be for?"

"Well," Sally began. "I suppose it's because I've finally found rest for my soul, like Katherine. I—" She paused, then with a tone of joyful confidence, said quietly, "I'm forgiven."

"Ah."

Katherine returned to the room in time to see Captain Braddock's warm smile.

"Welcome to the Old Paths, my girl."

13

An Eventful New Year

The days and weeks flew by in all the flurried rush of November and December, and almost before she knew it, Katherine awoke to the cold grey drizzle of a new year. Thinking over the past two months, Katherine wondered how it had all gone by so fast.

There had been the now yearly Guy Fawkes Day gathering, as well as the Thanksgiving dinner Mrs. James always hosted at the tea shop for anyone who didn't have family to celebrate with.

Katherine smiled and closed her eyes, reliving the cozy family-style meal. They had moved all the small tearoom tables together to make one long banquet table, and filled the counter with turkey, mashed potatoes, gravy, cranberry sauce, and all sorts of good things. Then even more food was brought in by the people who came in from across Harborhaven and the next two towns to enjoy Thanksgiving dinner together.

Sally had thrown herself into the preparations with energy. It was her first Thanksgiving, but she seemed determined that everything would be just right. She and Katherine whisked the dishes away to the kitchen as soon as everyone was finished, and spent the remainder of the evening chatting and laughing like old friends as they cleaned.

Then Katherine spent Christmas with her parents at their small house in the big city suburbs, relishing the joy of their newfound closeness after years of emotional distance. God had given her so many new beginnings in the past year, and reconciliation with her parents was one of the most significant.

Now, Katherine looked in the mirror by the front door of her apartment, twisting her long brown curls into a loose bun at the back of her head and smiling. Just when she felt she couldn't be more grateful for the changes God had worked in her heart, she found her heart even more filled with joy.

Descending the stairs, she paused for a moment in the pale blue light of the new day. *A new day, a new year.* Katherine stretched and padded softly into the kitchen to retrieve a leftover pasty. With the shop closed for New Year's Day and Sally with Mr. and Mrs. James in New York, the day stretched before her, refreshingly empty and serene, full of possibility, like the new year.

* * * *

After breakfast, Katherine curled up in the window seat with *Middlemarch*, but try as she might, she found it nearly impossible to keep her mind on the story. True, she had hit a dry patch in the narrative, but that wasn't really the reason. Her mind kept wandering back in time to the Harborside's "golden age," when the shop occupied the whole block of warehouses.

The long rectangle of Victorian brick had been built by Edward Braddock in 1890, but apart from those first few years, the Harborside had never been quite prosperous enough to warrant such a large space. As far as Katherine knew, the rest of the block had remained mostly empty in the years since the Braddocks sold the space, yet they had never been able to buy it back. *I wonder who owns it now.*

Katherine looked down at her book and sighed, starting the page again, but still unable to focus. *Maybe I'll go for a walk*, she thought. Tossing her book onto a side table, she flung the blankets into their basket and began bundling up for a cold, damp New Year stroll.

* * * *

Seagulls wheeled overhead as Katherine walked along the wharf. She looked across the harbor to where the dull grey of sky and water met in the distance. Even in the bleak days of winter, she still loved to walk along the wharf, the wooden boards sounding hollow under foot and the waves lapping against the pilings. The sights, the sounds, the smells, all were familiar and home-like.

As Katherine approached the Harborside, she surveyed the brick façade. *It looks in good condition.* she thought. *I wonder what it's like on the inside.*

* * * *

"Cap'n! Miss Katherine's here!" Tommy shouted as she gingerly tried the Harborside's doorknob and found it unlocked. She smiled and entered the shop, greeted by its familiar dusty fragrance.

"Well, then. I wondered if you would show up on yer day off." Captain Braddock limped into the shop holding an antique hatbox. "Yer just in time to help put the nativity pieces away."

"Sure! You're a day late, aren't you?" Katherine said with a wink. "What *would* Grandma Braddock say?"

Captain Braddock set the box on the counter with a chuckle. "She'd say we had better get to work." Turning, he called out, "Tommy, did you find that box down there?"

There was a faint mumble, and a thump, and a distant sound of falling cardboard.

"Oh, those must be the boxes I left down there last Thursday." Katherine headed towards the storeroom door.

"I'm ok." Tommy called up the stairs. "The big pile of boxes fell over, but they're empty anyway."

"Can you manage the box the Captain sent you for?" Katherine asked, peering down into the dim light of the storeroom.

"Yup." Tommy replied confidently.

"All right, then. Let me know if you want me to help."

"Yes, Ma'am."

Katherine returned to the shopfront and opened the hatbox. Taking out a piece of tissue paper, she picked up the shepherd from the nativity set and wound the tissue paper around him. Reaching for another piece, she suddenly stopped.

"Captain?"

"Yes, Katherine?" Captain Braddock looked up from the ornaments he was carefully removing from the tree in the window.

"The angel... it's here! Wherever did you find it?"

"Serena brought it when she came to visit last year. Said she kept it with her when she moved away as sort of a tie to the Harborside. She figured it would always give her a reason to come back."

"I suppose that explains why we couldn't find it last year."

They worked on in silence for a while, then Katherine ventured, "I was just wondering as I walked here this morning, do you know who owns the rest of the warehouses on this block?"

"I think the Braddocks originally sold to a friend who ran some sort of shipping company, but I've never heard about anyone selling it more recently, so it's probably still his, or his descendants, more likely. Not that they've done anything with it." Captain Braddock's brow furrowed up as he turned back to the box of ornaments.

"Here's the box!" Tommy triumphantly burst into the shop with the exuberance of a small boy who has just done something the grownups thought he couldn't.

The three worked cheerfully on. With Tommy's help, Captain Braddock got the ornaments put away and the tree taken out to the dumpster. Katherine took a few of the boxes down to the storeroom while the other two worked to take down the garlands from the windows.

As Katherine turned to start up the stairs, she heard a crash, a sickening thud, then a soft moan and a panicked yelp from Tommy. Heart racing, Katherine ran up the stairs and rounded the corner.

Captain Braddock lay motionless on the floor, bits of broken glass and pottery around him. A chair lay on its side nearby, and Tommy stood trembling by the door, eyes wide and pleading as he looked up at Katherine. Recognizing that he needed something to do, Katherine forced calmness into her tone and put her hand on his shoulder.

"Tommy, I need you to get a glass of water from the kitchen in case we need it."

Tommy nodded and dashed away.

"Captain?" Katherine knelt next to his motionless form and laid a hand on his chest. Relief flooded through her—he was still breathing.

"Is he..." Tommy asked from the doorway, glass of water spilling in his trembling hand.

"No, but I think he's hurt. Can you bring my bag from the coatrack?"

Tommy did, and Katherine rummaged for her phone, thankful for the unnatural calm that had settled over her in the wake of the initial shock. "Tommy, I'm going to call for help. I want you to go find the broom and dustpan and have them ready so we can clean up the broken glass and sharp things from the floor by him."

While they waited for the paramedics to arrive, Katherine and Tommy carefully cleared the broken shards and scattered tea leaves away from the floor where the captain still lay unconscious.

"Can't we put something under his head? It isn't nice to lie on the floor like that." Tommy's voice wavered, and tears filled his eyes.

"No, Tommy. We mustn't move him. I know it seems wrong to just leave him on the floor, but we don't know what's wrong. If we move him, we might hurt him more without realizing."

Tommy nodded, and a tear trickled down one cheek.

Katherine held out an arm. "Come sit by me. I'm sure help is almost here."

The boy sat next to her and buried his head in her shoulder. Katherine felt sobs shake his little body as she wrapped him in a hug, trying to stay strong for him. After a few minutes, the sobs subsided and Katherine broke the silence.

"Tommy, there is one thing we can do for the captain while we wait."

The boy lifted his tear-stained face, alert and ready for action. "What's that?"

"We can pray," Katherine said simply.

"I don't know how," Tommy dropped his head again.

"Then I'll pray out loud," Katherine said. Tommy clasped his hands together and squeezed his eyes shut.

"Lord, help Captain Braddock. Help him to wake up and help his injuries to heal. Help us to stay calm and be of whatever use we can. Show us how we can help him." Her voice broke and she had to pause for a while before finally whispering, "*Please*, in Jesus' name. Amen."

"Amen," Tommy echoed in a whisper, and the two clung tightly, eyes glued to the captain's face.

After several minutes, Katherine heard sirens in the

distance. At the same moment, Captain Braddock's lips parted and a low moan escaped.

"Captain?" Katherine said, gently putting Tommy to one side to free her arms. "Captain, can you hear me?"

"What..." the word was mumbled and barely recognizable. "Katherine..."

"Well, at least you know me." Katherine said, with an encouraging smile for Tommy.

"That...noise..."

"It's the paramedics, Captain. You've had a fall, and they've come to help." She squeezed his hand then turned to Tommy. "Go open the door and wave at them so they know where to go."

Tommy ran to the door and flung it open, the bell jingling raucously.

"Hang on, Captain. Help is here. You'll be all right." She gave the captain's hand another squeeze. *Lord, please let him be all right!*

* * * *

Katherine sat listening to the dull beep of the monitors and the soft hum of the nurses in the hallway outside. She had called Tommy's mom, who came to pick him up just after the captain was loaded into the ambulance. Since then, she sat by the captain's side while they ran tests and spoke in hushed tones, asking her what happened and how she was related to him.

They had called Serena, who had given the doctors permission to talk to Katherine about her brother's medical condition until she could get there. The captain himself drifted in and out of consciousness for a while, but now was soundly sleeping.

The doctors said he was suffering from a concussion, and would need to rest as much as possible. Their scans had also shown a broken bone in his ankle that required a splint for now, and a sturdier cast later on. Katherine felt she couldn't leave him there alone, especially since the doctors told her he was likely to experience some confusion and temporary issues with his memory as his brain healed from the concussion.

"Katherine?"

"I'm here. How are you feeling?" Katherine squeezed the captain's hand and leaned forward so he could see her better.

"I don't...what happened?"

"I didn't see, but Tommy said you fell."

"Tommy...is he ok?" His voice trailed off.

"Yes, he's just fine. His mom took him home." Katherine smiled and was thankful for a fresh wave of patience—this was the third time he had asked these same questions.

"My ankle hurts," he said, trying to sit up.

"Stay there." Katherine gently pushed his shoulder. He settled back into the pillows, and Katherine explained. "You broke your ankle when you fell. You also hit your head."

"Did I fall?"

"Yes." Katherine's heart squeezed. It pained her to see the confident, gruff captain so feeble and confused. *Lord, help him!* she prayed again. It was the only prayer her mind could form since the captain's fall, but it had become like breathing to her.

She watched as his eyes slowly drifted shut again and

wondered, *What would I do without him?* The thought filled her with dread, and she inched her chair just a little closer to the hospital bed.

She looked into his weathered face and remembered the first time she had met him. She would never have guessed that the gruff, distant man would end up so dear. She recalled his bluster about the Harborside being a family business, and her eyes filled with tears. He *was* family, maybe not by blood, but family, nonetheless.

Resting her forehead on his rough, wrinkled hand, she repeated the verse which she had been clinging to, feeling in deeper need than ever of its truth.

There is no fear in love...

14

Shipwrecked

Katherine slowly drifted awake in the dim light of the hospital room. Through sleep-bleared eyes, she peered around, unsure at first where she was. As her eyes cleared, she became aware of stiff legs and arms, and a back aching from being too long in an awkward position.

She gingerly straightened her legs and began to stretch. The chair she had curled up in was far from comfortable, but she hadn't wanted to leave the captain. He was still sleeping, so she stood and gingerly took a few steps around the room, trying to wake up her painfully tingling limbs.

Limping back to her chair, she moved it closer to the hospital bed and sat, watching the captain sleep, wondering how everything could change so completely in just an instant.

She looked at the clock on the wall and sighed. *Time to start the morning baking.* But there was no way she could leave the captain. Miss Harriet's would have to stay closed for now, as would the Harborside.

And then, what would she do later on, when the captain went home? Katherine knew he would need some care. Other than Serena, far away across the world, she was all he had. She would help him get around while his leg healed—but what about the shops? Her head spun and she felt her aching muscles tighten as she tried to figure out how to manage both shops and care for the captain.

Once she was certain the captain was sleeping soundly, she slipped out into the hallway to stretch her cramped legs. The nurses at the nearby station looked up briefly, then went back to their conversation as if she didn't exist. Katherine had never felt so alone. A wave of emotion threatened to engulf her there and then, but she took a breath and kept pacing to wake up her legs.

Standing in the doorway so she could keep an eye on the captain, she pulled out her phone to check for messages. A flicker of relief—Serena was coming. And Sally would arrive in the afternoon—she could help keep Miss Harriet's limping along.

Leaning against the doorway of the captain's room, she remembered her conversation with Mrs. James the night before.

"Sally will be there tomorrow. I've given her the keys to my car so you two will be mobile."

"Thank you."

"Katherine,"

"Yes?"

"I think I should cancel the rest of the trip."

Katherine's heart squeezed in her chest. As much as she

longed for her friend to be there with her, she couldn't let her give up the long-awaited trip to her childhood home. "No. You can't... you've been looking forward to it for so long, and your brother's expecting you!"

"I know. But I can't leave the whole burden of *my* tea shop on your shoulders while I go off to England to enjoy myself, especially at such a time."

"I'll have Sally."

There was a long pause.

"Is it *enough*, Dearie? Will you be able to manage with just Sally to help?"

Katherine had silently prayed before giving an answer.

"I think so."

"Our flight leaves at nine tomorrow evening. Will you promise to call me right away if you decide you need me home?"

"I promise."

"Good girl."

Katherine's heart warmed at the matronly tone that felt like a hug.

"How I wish I could be there with you, Katherine. I can't imagine how hard this is, and all of us so far away."

Tears had trickled down Katherine's cheeks.

"You know you can call me at any time, even in England. And I'll be praying for you."

"Thank you." She had barely managed a whisper.

The steady beeping of the monitor slowly brought her back to the present. Captain Braddock's forehead creased in a frown as he drifted awake.

"Good morning." Katherine said softly, returning to her chair by his bedside.

"Katherine."

"Do you know where you are?" she asked trying to smile.

"It...appears...I'm in a hospital." He said haltingly, trying to raise a hand tethered by an IV and oximeter.

Freeing the cords from where they had gotten tangled, she waited for the question, praying it wouldn't come this time.

"What happened?'

Here we go again.

* * * *

No matter how many angles she considered it from, she came to the same conclusion. Someone needed to go deal with the Harborside's deliveries. They had a shipment of Puer-Sheng coming, along with more Assam and the boxes of teabags for Miss Harriet's.

She glanced at the captain, trying to gauge how soon he would be awake. Sally's flight had landed and she was on her way from the airport in Mrs. James' car. If she could get to the Harborside by three, she would be there when the deliveries came. It was too cold and damp for the boxes to be sitting out on the step. The tea always came carefully packaged, but still.

The weight of responsibility made her stomach feel tight, as another wave of loneliness swept over her. She had to figure this out, to keep things together. *Lord, help me!* She prayed.

* * * *

"Hi." Sally smiled shyly as Katherine got in the car.

"Hi." Katherine tried to smile back.

"How is he?"

"Asleep. He sleeps a lot right now. I'm hoping to be back before he wakes up. The nurses said they would call if I'm needed or if he asks for me."

"Is he...going to be okay?"

"Yes, he should be, but the doctors say it's going to take some time."

"What can I do?"

Katherine recognized in her friend's face the same frightened helplessness she had been feeling. "Pray."

"I am. Anything else?"

"Yes. After you drop me off at the Harborside, could you go to Miss Harriet's and make sure we have everything we need for tomorrow?"

"Sure. When should I pick you up again?"

"Probably four. In case the delivery comes late."

"Ok. Want me to prep the pasty filling for tomorrow? I should have time."

"That would be great." Katherine let out a long breath and actually managed a smile as her friend pulled up to the curb outside the Harborside's green door. "Thank you, Sally."

"Happy to help."

* * * *

The familiar jingle of the bell over the door jarred the silence of the old building as Katherine walked in. She picked up the broom and dustpan from where Tommy had flung them in his rush to be helpful and walked over to the shelves.

He had done a good job of sweeping up, but there were still a few fragments of pottery that had bounced further away. As she bent to retrieve one, something caught her eye behind the curve of the spiral staircase. She took a step nearer and felt her breath catch in her chest.

No, not that too! She stooped to pick up the *Anne* from where it lay, a mass of tangled rigging and broken spars. All the pent-up emotion of the last two days welled up in Katherine's heart, and she wept.

She felt she had been shipwrecked, too, left to struggle alone, clinging to the last shattered remnants of all that was dear and familiar. Sinking to her knees, she held the broken pieces of the *Anne* to her and let the tears fall, mourning the loss of such a precious symbol of so many generations of Braddock history. She wondered how the captain would take the news of this tragedy, and dreaded having to repeat the loss over and over till his concussion healed.

Shivering, she suddenly realized how cold it felt in the empty shop. She stood and laid what remained of the Anne on the counter, then rushed over to the thermometer. *68. At least the tea is all right.* She went to a bookshelf in the Captain's Quarters and took down a box, revealing an old dial thermostat. She turned it up some, and heard the ticking of the ornate cast iron radiator in the corner.

Entering the shop, Katherine switched on the lights and the warm, rosy glow of the old converted gas lights filled the shop with visual warmth. She knelt in front of the wood stove, and felt herself stiffen. She had never lit the fire herself.

Taking a breath, she closed her eyes and breathed out her new favorite prayer: *"Lord, please help."*

She picked up the metal dustpan and brush and cleared out the ashes of the New Year's Day fire, taking note of where the charred remains of the logs had been. Then, she arranged the wood and kindling as she had seen the captain do, and soon the fire was blazing away.

She left the door open and leaned her head against the arm of the chair, as she had done the day the captain told the last of the *Anne*'s story. A new wave of loss and anxiety swept over her.

The Anne. How was she ever going to tell the captain?

15

Hope for the Harborside

Katherine glanced up from *Middlemarch* the next morning to see a tall lady with dark, silver-streaked hair leaning on the doorframe and looking in with loving compassion in her weary eyes.

"Serena!" Katherine jumped up and hurried to greet the captain's sister with a hug. Remembering to speak softly, she whispered, "I can't believe you got here so soon!"

"I was able to find a flight out right away. I didn't tell you, because travel can be so unpredictable this time of year, and I didn't know when I would actually arrive." Turning towards the bed, she asked, "How is he doing?"

"Doctor says he'll be released this afternoon."

"And the concussion?"

"He's sleeping a lot, and still asking the same questions over and over, but the doctors said that's fairly normal at first."

"I can't tell you how glad I am you were there when it

happened, and that you stayed with him." She smiled sympathetically and nodded toward the blanket tucked into a corner of the chair. "Have you even been home at all?"

Katherine shook her head. "Just to the Harborside, to clean things up and bring in the deliveries. I didn't want the tea shipments left out in the cold and rain."

Serena smiled and shook her head. "Are you sure there isn't a Braddock hiding somewhere in your family tree?"

The two chuckled, and Katherine felt for the first time in days that perhaps all was not as dismal as it had felt. Sally was at Miss Harriet's, and now Serena would help with the captain.

While Serena watched for her brother to wake up again, Katherine went out into the hall to ask the nurses for another chair. Finding a space in the corner that seemed more or less out of the way, Katherine set the chair down and curled up in it. Serena had taken the chair by the captain's bed, picking up Katherine's book.

"Is it good?" She handed it back to Katherine with a smile.

"I didn't think so at first, but it gets better about halfway through."

"I'll keep that in mind. I've never read it, but have always thought I should."

"Serena?" The captain's eyes had drifted open and he stared at Serena in disbelief. "I must be bad off...if you've come all the way here."

"Of course I came. Couldn't leave Katherine to deal with my crotchety brother all alone, now, could I?" Serena said teasingly, giving his hand a gentle squeeze.

"Katherine—"

"I'm here." Katherine came from her corner and stood on the other side of the captain's bed.

"I'm blessed indeed," he said with a weak smile. "That bump on my head might just have been worth it after all to have my two favorite people waiting on me."

Katherine's eyes grew wide. "You remember?"

"Not exactly. But when I woke up before, you told me that I hit my head."

Serena gave a little clap. "Well done!"

Captain Braddock frowned. "What's the fuss about?

"That's the first time you've woken up and remembered." Katherine gave a shy half-smile. "Before, you just kept asking what happened over and over."

"That sounds pretty tedious. I'm sorry to put you through that, Missy."

"I don't mind now. I'm just so happy you're on the mend." Katherine blinked, hoping the captain couldn't see the tears brimming in her eyes.

"I'll be right as rain in no time, just you wait."

"I think you'll be the one waiting, Jeremiah." Serena put on a matter-of-fact tone. The doctor says you have to rest and stay off your ankle for six weeks." Serena gave him a stern look. "And I plan to make sure you follow doctor's orders."

* * * *

Steam, warm water, the scent of floral dish soap. Sally nearby, rummaging for a dish towel.

All's right with the world—at least for the moment. Katherine smiled.

"Didn't you say it's a big place? How did you manage to get him inside?"

"Serena went through the house and opened a door that led out onto their garden walk. Apparently it's some sort of study or something next to one of the ground floor bedrooms. We were able to wheel him right in."

"That's a mercy." Sally pushed the curtain to one side and went out into the tearoom.

"Yes, it really was." Katherine swished the dish soap around to dissolve it and turned off the tap. "There is so much of God's mercy in this." She breathed a silent prayer of thanks as Sally wheeled the cart into the kitchen.

"It could have been worse, you know," she continued. "The concussion could have been more severe, or he could have been alone when it happened—I struggled to see it at the time, but now I can see God's hand in it."

Sally placed a stack of plates on the counter. "Why *was* he on a chair, anyway?"

"Tommy said he put chair there for himself, to get one last garland hanger they had left on the window. But he couldn't reach, even with the chair, so the captain stepped up and then just sort of crumpled. The doctor said his blood pressure probably dipped, like when you stand up too quick and get dizzy. Apparently that happens easily to older people.

"Anyway, his hand must have flailed out and hit the shelves as he fell. Some of the tea bowls were broken and—"

Katherine looked down, swiping her rag around and around the plate in her hand. Her throat felt tight and a flood of emotion squeezed her stomach. Finally, she managed to whisper, "the *Anne*... I found the *Anne* smashed on the floor."

"Oh, Katherine. Not the *Anne!*" Sally laid a comforting hand on Katherine's arm. "How did the captain take it?"

"I haven't told him yet." They worked on in silence for a while.

"I know it's just a model ship, but I can't help but feel the loss of it. It's such a symbol of the Harborside, of the Braddocks. The tea bowls were probably more valuable, but the *Anne* is more...important."

"I know."

Katherine looked up. Sally's eyes met hers, full of compassion and understanding. Katherine smiled and put all her heart in the words Mrs. James had said to them so often:

"I'm glad you're here."

* * * *

Jolted awake by her alarm the next morning, Katherine's first thoughts were of the captain. She wanted to go see how he was doing, but the responsibilities of both shops required a full day's time and attention. *Lord, I know Serena will take care of him. But please, help him, and heal him."*

Sitting up and pushing back the covers, she added, *And please help me, too."*

* * * *

"Now, after we finish setting the tables, I'll check the tea drawers to see what I need to bring back from the Harborside today. Did you check the supplies in the kitchen?"

"Yes. I did. We're fine for today, but we'll need to order flour, cream, and eggs for tomorrow."

"I'll call about that today while I'm at the Harborside."

They wheeled the cart to the last table and began setting out the dishes.

"I know you've handled the kitchen side of things before, but are you sure you'll be ok with the customers too?"

"I'll do my best."

Katherine thought Sally seemed unusually calm as she placed the last of the silverware on the table. "You haven't dropped a thing this morning, and you seem...well...settled. What's different?"

A shy smile spread across Sally's face as she said simply, "I've been prayin'." And turned to push the cart back to the kitchen.

This just might work. Katherine thought, a glow of hope beginning to warm her heart as she watched Sally walk away.

* * * *

The Harborside felt too quiet as Katherine flipped the sign to "*Open*" and tugged the dark green window shade, noticing for the first time the whirring sound it made as it wound itself up. She had worked at the Harborside for over two years now, but never a whole day without the captain.

She stooped to adjust the door and check on the fire she had just made in the wood stove. *Still burning. Good.*

Glancing over at the counter, she sighed. She should probably find something to put the broken pieces of the *Anne* in so they wouldn't get lost. Listening for the bell in case a customer ventured in, she went down into the storeroom and sifted through the pile of empty boxes Tommy had knocked over. *If only that had been the only mishap that day*, she thought.

Once she found a box that looked the right size, she jogged up the stairs again. Gingerly, she picked up the tangled mass of lines and rigging. She didn't know much about ships, but it looked to her like two of the masts were snapped off. Several pieces of decking also seemed to be gone. Katherine walked around the staircase, examining the floor to see if she had missed them. *I hope Tommy or I didn't throw them away when we swept the floor.*

She was on her hands and knees behind the spiral staircase when she heard the bell ring.

A tall, thin man stood near the counter, brushing raindrops from his short silvery hair.

"Mr. Patten! I didn't expect to see you today. How are you?" She stood and dusted her hands off as she walked over to greet the elderly bank manager.

"I'm well, thank you, Katherine. I was on my way to work and saw you were open again. So sorry to hear about the captain's accident. Is he recovering well?"

"Yes. He came home from the hospital yesterday. His sister is taking care of him."

"Serena is here?"

"Yes, and I'm so thankful she was able to get here so quickly."

"I actually have something I need to speak to her and the captain about, only I didn't know she was in town. That's why I stopped by, actually. I heard about the captain's accident, and figured you could tell me if he were up to talking with me. You see, something strange happened at the bank yesterday."

* * * *

"How did it go?" Katherine asked as she stepped in from the cold January rain and flipped the sign from *"Do Come In"* to *"Come Again Soon."*

"I can't say for sure. It was all a bit of a blur, and I'm ever so tired now."

Katherine chuckled. "That sounds about right. But if the place is still standing and so are you, I'd say you probably did just fine. I'll grab the cart and start clearing the tables."

Sally flopped into a chair. "Thanks," she said, a bit breathlessly. "There was an odd rush right at the end. Thought they'd never all leave."

Katherine rolled the cart to the first table and started sorting, scraping and stacking dishes. Sally got reluctantly to her feet to join her.

"I have it good over at the Harborside." Katherine said with a chuckle. "I only have to stand up when a customer comes in."

"And how often is that?"

"It depends on the day. With such a drenching rain today, there were only a few customers—and Mr. Patten."

"I like him. He's a good egg."

"A good what?"

Sally shook her head with a laugh. "Never mind. What kind of tea did he get? His usual Earl Grey?"

"No, oddly enough, he didn't come in for tea. He wanted to see if I thought the captain well enough to discuss a business opportunity." Katherine felt a grin stretch across her face, despite her attempt to be serious.

"Now, what may that grin be about, then?" Sally brandished a teaspoon menacingly. "Out with it!"

"Oh, Sally, it's something I've been praying about, but didn't think could ever happen! And it's still not for sure."

"Well, what is it?"

Katherine pulled out a chair and sat, motioning for Sally to do the same. "Mr. Patten said that a man came into the bank today to clear out his uncle's safety deposit box. The man who owns the rest of the Harborside block has died, and it was his executor—a nephew or something—who came to the bank today."

"What's that got to do with you?" Sally asked, brow crumpled in confusion.

"When he opened the safety deposit box, there was a paper folded around the deed to the building. The man read it, then asked who these Braddocks were, and where he could find them."

"What? Why?"

"Because—" Katherine leaned forward and dropped her voice to an excited whisper. "The paper was the purchase contract for the Harborside block, and it stipulates that if ever the property is sold, it must first be offered to the Braddocks before being placed on the market."

"Do you think they'll be able to buy it?" Sally asked, eyes wide.

"I don't know." Katherine sat back against her chair with a frown. "But for some reason, this very thing has been on my heart for months—the Braddocks owning the whole block like they used to—and I've been praying about it, so this can't be a coincidence. I'm going to stop by to see the captain when we're done here, and I'll talk to Serena about it then."

16

Worth a Try

"Yes, Mr. Welch called us this afternoon. Apparently, he's in quite a hurry to sell."

"And?" Katherine held her breath.

"Oh, Katherine, whatever would we do with the whole block? We don't even use half the storeroom."

Katherine let out her breath. She was ready for this question. "Well, I've been thinking we could open a museum. It would honor the Braddock family legacy and bring in customers at the same time."

A smile spread over Serena's face and her eyes sparkled. "I think that's a wonderful idea, Katherine!" but just as quickly, her face clouded. "There's just one problem."

"The money?"

Serena nodded. "You've seen the books. The Harborside is well out of danger financially, but nowhere near ready to make such a large purchase. Unless—" Katherine watched as the older woman's face took on an odd, faraway look.

"Unless what?"

Serena motioned for her to sit down next to her on the small couch and turned to face her. "When I was young, Granny Braddock used to talk about a trust, that she would turn over to me when I was old enough. She said it was set aside by Isaac and Lizzy Braddock—"

"Lizzy who gave the Harborside its bell?"

"You have been paying attention. Yes, that's her. Well, the Harborside didn't come to them, you see. Isaac being a middle child, the shop's ownership went to the oldest, my great-grandfather, Henry."

"I never knew that. I guess I assumed that because they're part of the Harborside's story, it must have belonged to them."

"No, Isaac and Lizzy only worked there. Henry Braddock, who as I understand was a good man who worked hard and tried to keep the Harborside going, ended up having to choose between bankruptcy and selling the warehouse spaces Edward had built around the original building."

"How horrible. I can't imagine making such a difficult decision." Katherine said, realizing she had assumed the rest of the block had been lost due to some carelessness or unconcern. "But you said something about Isaac and Lizzie?"

"Yes. Henry didn't tell them about having to sell until it was already done. Thankfully, he put that bit into the contract about offering it to the Braddock family first before selling it. When Isaac and Lizzy found out, they decided to make certain that the building would one day be recovered."

"How?"

"Lizzy had a bit of money settled on her when she married, and Isaac had a few savings as well. They both agreed to put that money away, and add to it as they could. They put their little fund into a trust, and, according to Granny, each generation has added to it. If she was right, there *is* money to buy the building, but I don't know how much or even where it is."

"But if she told you about it—"

"Just before she died, she told me she had taken care of the papers, and that the trust was now in my name. I didn't understand what she meant at the time, but now I wonder if there might be papers somewhere that tell who I need to talk to in order to withdraw the funds and buy the building."

Katherine's eyes lit up. "The sea chests! We've only just started sorting through the papers in your grandmother's chest. I'm sure it's in there, if it's anywhere."

The sparkle returned to Serena's eyes. "It may well be!"

* * * *

The next morning, Katherine unlocked the door to the Harborside, feeling as if she were about to embark upon a grand adventure. She opened the wood stove and cleaned out the remnants of yesterday's fire, then laid a new fire and lit a long match.

Once she was satisfied that the fire wasn't going to die out, she hurried to the captain's desk and pulled out a drawer. There lay a heavy, ornate iron key, just like what Katherine had always imagined the key to the Secret Garden would have looked like.

When she first came to the Harborside, Captain Braddock

had strictly forbidden "snooping," as he called it, and Katherine struggled hard against the temptation. But now—her heart gave a little leap at the thought—she had Serena's permission to snoop as much as she liked!

Of course, the captain had become quite open about the Harborside's secrets, over the last year, especially once Serena returned. *After all,* Katherine thought with a chuckle, *Serena was the Harborside's biggest secret for a while there.*

As she climbed the tight round spiral staircase, she reveled in what she was about to do. Unlocking the door, she pushed it open and stood still for a moment in the blue-grey dimness. Clouds had rolled in from the harbor, covering the hidden tower with a dense fog.

Her eyes were drawn to the oldest sea chest, the one that had belonged to the first Captain Braddock, but she tore her gaze away and knelt to open the newest chest instead.

She picked up a messy stack of jumbled papers and headed back downstairs, pulling the door closed, but not bothering to lock it. Then, settling herself down by the fire, she picked up the first few pieces of paper and looked them over. *Receipt. Receipt. Bill.*

* * * *

"How's it going?" Serena asked, pulling up a second chair by the captain's bed.

"Nothing yet, but I brought a box of papers for us to sort through here. I thought it might be faster with three of us."

"Good idea, Katherine." Captain Braddock said, shifting himself gingerly to sit straighter on his pillows.

"Now, Jeremiah, the doctor said you shouldn't be reading quite yet."

"If I didn't have such a headache, I'd probably argue with you." he leaned back on his pillows and closed his eyes. "But don't let me keep you two from it. Imagine, the whole Harborside block..." he smiled weakly and opened his eyes. "All right, then, what are you waiting for?"

Katherine and Serena reached into the box and began sorting.

"Recipe for some sort of sauce...Hard to read. Does that say 'breadcrumbs'?"

"Is it really? That must be the bread sauce your grandmother used to make at Christmas. I'll put it with the other recipes I've collected here."

"*Bread* sauce?" Serena raised an eyebrow.

"I didn't remember it either, till I had it at yer friend Harriet's house, last Christmas. It was the sauce Grandma made us put on our turkey, remember? White, and sorta lumpy."

Serena wrinkled her nose. "Oh, yes. I do remember. It wasn't my favorite, though."

"You should have Harriet make it for you sometime.—But don't you go tellin' her I recommended it."

Serena laughed. "You, Jeremiah, are most certainly back to your old curmudgeonly self."

* * * *

Two days later, Katherine stared into the half-full chest. *How could anyone leave behind so many papers?* A silvery jingle called her back to the storefront. Instead of one of their usual customers, Katherine saw the welcome sight of Tommy standing by the counter, wearing a puffy green jacket. Katherine recognized it as the one his mother bought for him just after she came to Harborhaven. It had been ridiculously large on him then, but as his mother predicted, he had grown into it and now it fit quite well.

"Can I be here?" he asked, glancing uncertainly around the shop.

"Of course, Tommy, why would you think you couldn't?"

"Because the cap'n isn't here..." his head drooped, and his fingers toyed with the zipper of his jacket as he whispered, "and 'cuz he fell off *my* chair."

"Oh, Tommy." Katherine wrapped the boy, coat and all, in the biggest hug she could muster. "You weren't the reason he fell."

"Really?" Tommy quickly swiped at a tear, which Katherine pretended not to have seen.

"Really. The doctors said he probably just stepped up there a bit too fast, and it made his blood pressure dip."

"What does that mean?"

"Never mind. It means it wasn't you or your chair or anything you could have helped."

"Then it's really ok?" Tommy looked up into her eyes, still skeptical.

"Yes, really and truly ok." She mussed the boy's hair like the captain always did. "Now, how about some help dusting the jars?"

"Ok!"

* * * *

The day flew by, with just enough customers to keep Katherine from feeling too sedentary as she went from the captain's desk to the storefront and back again. In the late afternoon there was a lull, and Katherine smiled as she looked over the day's figures in the old leatherbound ledger the captain used to track the Harborside's sales and expenses. Even in the bluster and biting cold of early January, the Harborside was holding her own.

"Miss Katherine," Tommy's voice held a question.

"Yes, Tommy?" Katherine walked to the doorway and poked her head around the door. "What is it?"

"Where's the cap'n's ship?" He pointed to the now empty shelf where the *Anne* used to sit.

Katherine took a deep breath and held it for a moment, deciding what to say. Finally, she let her breath out in a sigh and motioned Tommy over.

"Come and see." she moved behind the counter and pulled out the box.

"Is that...But it's broken!" Tommy stared, wide-eyed and dismayed.

"Yes. It happened when the captain had his fall."

Tommy moved close and whispered, "Can he fix it?"

She reached an arm around his shoulders and gave a quick squeeze as she whispered back, "I hope so."

* * * *

"Permission to come aboard?" Katherine asked softly as she stood at the captain's door that evening.

"Permission granted. Come on in." Nodding toward the box in her hands, he asked, "Did you bring more papers for Serena to sort through?"

"Not exactly. How are you tonight?" Katherine asked, helping adjust the pillows as he struggled to sit up.

"I suppose I'm a fair bit better, now you've come to see me." The captain smiled and gave her a playful wink.

"I'm glad to help, though you may not be so cheerful once I show you what I've brought."

The captain's brow furrowed. "Oh?"

Katherine brought the box closer and tipped it. She felt she should say something, but found there were simply no words. She watched the emotions sweep across the captain's face: shock, anger, sorrow, disappointment. He stared into the box.

"How—"

"When you fell."

He reached a hand toward the jumbled pieces, then drew it back again, as if afraid to touch it and make the loss real.

"Serena said some things were broken." He looked up at her.

Katherine nodded. "Some of the tea bowls."

"Well, they were valuable, but not irreplaceable." He sighed heavily. "Not like the *Anne* here."

They sat in silence while the wind battered the window-pane with raindrops and moaned through the eaves of the old house.

"Tommy came by today. It was the first time since your accident."

"How is he?"

"I think he's ok now... He'd been feeling like he was to blame for your fall."

"Poor lad! And does he still think that?"

Katherine smiled. "No. We had a talk, and he seems back to his old self now."

"Good." Captain Braddock looked down at the ship in front of him with a thoughtful look on his face. Then, he began gently sifting through the pieces. "Go to the closet there, will you Katherine, and bring me the long wooden box up on the shelf."

"What's this?" she asked, bringing the box, which looked a little like a smaller version of one of the sea chests at the Harborside.

"William Braddock's woodworking tools. They've been passed down as somewhat of an heirloom, along with a bit of his skill."

"You mean, you know how to use all these?" Katherine felt a thrill of wonder as he raised the lid and she looked over the antique tools, the dark wood of their handles bearing the smooth polish that comes with generations of use.

"I know just about enough to get along." Captain Braddock said, pulling the tray out of the box and rummaging through an assortment of pieces of wood, all different shapes and sizes.

"What are you looking for?"

"A new mast. Braddocks tend to hold on to things, if you hadn't noticed by now. There might be a piece in here I could use to repair or remake the main mast. But I'll have to take the rigging apart to see what else is amiss."

"Do you think she can be repaired?" Katherine asked, feeling a glimmer of hope.

"Maybe. It's worth a try, anyway." He glanced up at Katherine. "It's always worth a try."

17

Peach Tea and Kindness

"Katherine, have you noticed anything strange about Rosie this week?" Sally took a batch of scones out of the oven and replaced it with a pan of pasties.

"No, but I haven't really seen her. I've been out the door before anyone gets here in the mornings, and she doesn't usually stay till closing time. What have you noticed?"

"Well, you know that fake injured air she puts on when she comes in here now?"

"Yes."

"Well, the past few days, she hasn't been like that. She seems to be genuinely sad."

Katherine reached up into the china cupboard and pulled out a cup and saucer. "Have you asked her what's wrong?"

Sally frowned down at the scones she was placing on a rack to cool. "I don't think she'd tell me. After all, she's never liked me, and after that day when we blew up at each other,

I've just ignored her best as I can." Setting the empty pan on the counter, she got out a mixing bowl and spoon. "If Auntie H. were here, she would know exactly what to do."

"That's true." Katherine put a couple scoops of loose tea into the diffuser of a teapot she was prepping for Mrs. Penelope's very predictable daily order. "Do you remember what she told us that first day after the blow-up, when Rosie came back in?"

Sally put her hands on her hips. "Yes, that our job was to be '*Kind*, you hear?'"

Katherine laughed at her friend's imitation of Mrs. James' stern tone. "Yes, that. Well, if you want to find out what's wrong, maybe you just need to find a way to be extra kind to her."

Sally's eyes lit up with interest. "How?"

"I don't know... I haven't thought it out that far yet." Katherine glanced up at the clock on the wall. "I should get over to the Harborside, but I do think you're on the right track." She chuckled. "It's funny for the two of us to be talking about Rosie like this, instead of complaining."

"I guess that's the difference forgiveness makes," Sally slowly picked up a batter bowl and set it in the sink. "I never would have cared before if Rosie were sad or not."

"But now?"

"Now, it *matters*. I don't know why, but I just know it matters, and that I'm the one who's supposed to do something about it."

"Then pray. God will help." Katherine took her apron off and hung it on the old coatrack they used as an "apron tree." Halfway to the door, she suddenly stopped and walked back to the kitchen "And Sally," she said, peeking around the curtain, "Try giving her peach tea—with honey."

* * * *

*Inventory...ordering... Tommy will help dust the jars later...Ledger is up to date...*Katherine scanned the to-do list she had hurriedly scrawled that morning. She finally felt caught up on the Harborside's normal tasks. Now it was time to sort through another stack of papers from the trunk. She put the kettle on in the small hidden kitchen and stopped at the desk for the key to the secret tower and the box she had used to carry a stack of papers the day before.

Mounting the staircase had lost some of its excitement over the past few days, especially since a new excitement had taken the limelight on the stage of Katherine's imagination. Sorting through the papers was tedious at times, but it still held all the thrill and promise of a real-life treasure hunt.

Reaching down, she worked her fingers into the scattered mass, glad to see the trunk noticeably emptier than the day before. As she lifted a messy stack, an envelope fell out and landed on the floor. Sliding the papers into the waiting box, she bent to pick up the envelope. *Return to sender...* She flipped it over. *It hasn't been opened.*

She peered at the shaky handwriting. It looked like Grandma Braddock's writing, and it was addressed from the Harborside. The "Return to sender" covered the first name of the recipient, but the last name and address were readable. *Strange.* Katherine frowned. *It's addressed to a Braddock...* but she had thought there were no other Braddocks left, apart from the captain and Serena.

Her fingers itched to open the letter, but instead she deliberately stuffed it underneath the papers in her box. She would ask Serena about the letter later on. After all, they were looking for paperwork about the trust, not family correspondence. The prize of restoring the Harborside's lost warehouse still seemed so far away.

* * * *

"How did you know?" Sally asked as Katherine slipped through the kitchen curtain that evening.

"How did I know what?" Katherine flung an apron strap over her head and tied the strings while Sally squirted soap into the sink.

"About the peach tea and honey for Rosie? I mean, how d'you just look at someone and *know* what they'd like?"

"Magic." Katherine winked, gently nudging Sally over and taking her place at the sink.

Sally took a dishrag from the drawer and threw it at her, before grabbing a towel for herself. "I know very well it's nothing of the kind. So how do you know? Or is it some secret you can't tell me?"

"It isn't a secret." Katherine said, watching the foamy bubbles rise as the sink filled. "Just difficult to explain."

"Well can you try? I've seen you and Auntie H. do it, and I want to know how."

"I just sort of picked it up from watching the captain, and

she picked it up from watching me, although I think she was already naturally good at reading people."

"Reading people... but how do you *know*, what do you look for?"

"Little things... At first, I just paid attention to the Dailies, like Mr. James and Mrs. Penelope." Katherine handed Sally a plate to dry. "I thought about what they ordered, what their personalities were like, what kinds of things they liked or disliked, and then as I learned about the different teas, I just had a hunch they would like a certain kind."

"So I need to learn about the different teas." Sally frowned. She finished drying the plate and set it on a shelf in the cupboard.

"That would be a start. But you don't have to study them, just notice things as you make different kinds of tea for people. Notice how each tea smells, whether or not people tend to put milk or sugar in it, what kinds of people really enjoy it. It's mostly a matter of observation."

"Well, you must be good at observing, because that tea really opened Rosie up."

"Really?"

"Yes. She came in looking sad, like she has been, and so I brought out the tea and said that you thought she would like it, and to be sure to put honey in it."

"And?" Katherine handed Sally a pink floral teacup before sliding its matching saucer into the dish water.

"She looked like she didn't know what to do at first." Sally reached for the saucer and looked down with a blush as she dried it. "I suppose she isn't used to me being nice to her."

"Maybe not." Katherine bent her head to catch her friends' eye. "But I'm proud of you for being kind to her today."

A soft smile came across Sally's face.

"What happened next?"

"I went over after a while and asked if she liked the tea. She actually *smiled* at me, Katherine!"

"Wow. I haven't seen her smile at anyone in weeks."

"I know. Well, later on, when she asked for her check, I said it was on the house today."

"And what did she say?"

"She gave me a sort of sideways look—suspicious, like—and asked why."

Katherine chuckled. "That sounds more like Rosie. What did you tell her?"

"I just said I had noticed her looking sad of late, and hoped to cheer her up."

"And how did she react to that?"

"Her eyes got all swimmy and she said, 'thank you' and started rummaging in her bag for a hankie. I went off for a bit, but when she stood to leave, I went over and said, 'Have a good day, Rosie.' And she smiled again a little."

"That's certainly progress."

"Yes. The only problem is, I can't give her free tea and scones every day. So what should I do next?"

"I think it was more your gentleness that won the day, rather than the tea itself. Just keep being kind, and God will show you what's next."

Sally suddenly giggled. "You sounded exactly like Auntie H. when you said that."

"Why, thank you! Must be the dish soap. It makes you wiser."

"Is that so? Well, in that case, I'll wash, you dry." She gave Katherine a playful push and tossed the dish towel at her.

"I guess I should have seen that coming," Katherine said with a rueful smile.

* * * *

When the dishes were done and everything prepped for the next day, Katherine took the box of papers over to the Braddock's house. She paused on the doorstep and looked up at the sky.

The stormy clouds that had drenched Harborhaven all day had blown off somewhere else, and the clear sky glimmered with stars. Even the gleam of the porchlight couldn't blot them out, and Katherine stood gazing, not quite ready to pull herself away from the scene.

She let the peacefulness of the crisp night seep into her. It had been awhile since she had taken time to be still like this, just staring up at the stars, breathing out soft puffs of cloud into the frigid night air.

She thought of that evening on the wharf when she asked God to help her get the rest of the Harborside block back. Looking down at the box in her arms, which was just beginning to feel heavy, she closed her eyes and prayed again.

Lord, so much is happening. You have brought the owner's executor here at exactly this time to make this offer. Please help us find the information we need, and please help the trust to have enough money to buy back the warehouses.

Opening her eyes, she climbed the steps to the front door of the Braddock's Victorian mansion and rang the bell.

"Katherine, come in. Jeremiah's napping, but I'd enjoy some company. Did you bring more papers to sort?" Serena ushered her into the hall which always struck Katherine with a sense of grandeur. A wide wooden staircase spiraled up to the left of the door, reminding Katherine of the Harborside's much smaller staircase.

She stopped and looked up through the middle of the staircase as Serena continued down the hall toward the small sitting room. She had seen this house from the outside all her life, and always wanted to see what the inside looked like. Although she had been in the stately old mansion many times now, she hadn't stopped to really look around until this moment. Oh, how she wanted to explore!

"Coming?" Serena asked, an amused smile crinkling up the corners of her eyes.

"Yes. I was just admiring the staircase."

"It is beautiful, isn't it? But then, I might be biased."

"Braddocks do seem to be partial to spiral staircases," Katherine said with a laugh.

"Oh, yes. And this one was designed to be especially grand."

"Edward again?"

"You've been paying attention." Serena smiled at Katherine before letting her eyes trace the wide curve of the staircase. He built this just before the Harborside's brick façade went up. The Braddock's original home was plain and simple, and much smaller."

"Like the old farmhouses that used to stand where Cliffton is?"

"Yes, in fact, it was essentially just like those. After Anne and Jeremiah died, Edward decided to pull down the house, which as you can imagine caused great consternation among the rest of the Braddocks."

This sparked Katherine's memory and she hurried to set her box on a chair and retrieve the unopened letter. "I haven't found anything about the trust, but I did find this today." she handed the letter to Serena. "It looked intriguing."

Serena turned the letter over slowly in her hands. "That's Granny Braddock's writing, for sure." She squinted at the address on the front. "But, does that really say *Braddock*?... And in such a faraway place as New York!"

"I wondered why it was never opened."

"Yes, that is odd." Serena's hand hovered over the flap for a moment, then she looked up at Katherine. "We should wait for Jeremiah. He would want to be here when we open it, especially if it means there's another Braddock somewhere."

Serena set the letter down on a small table beside the captain's favorite armchair, saying softly to herself, "Maybe we aren't the last ones left, after all."

18

The Letter

The time had finally come. Serena and Katherine leaned nearer to the captain's chair, heads bent close, eyes alight with anticipation. The cozy glow of the fireplace mingled with soft light from a number of table lamps scattered throughout the room, making it feel warm and welcoming, but echoing the mysteriousness of the unopened letter.

Captain Braddock flipped the envelope over to examine the address. "Yer right. It is certainly to a Braddock, and in New York." Picking up an antique silver letter opener Serena had set beside the letter, he slid the long, thin blade under the flap.

The room was still. No one moved or breathed, and the only sounds were the ticking of the mantel clock and the soft tearing of paper. Unfolding the letter, the captain held it up to Serena. "I think you should read it out to us, since this light makes it hard on my eyes."

Serena nodded, took the age-yellowed paper in her hands, and began to read.

"September 8, 1948.

Dear Sir,

I thank you for your letter. It was a shock to read such bitter allegations about Captain Jeremiah Braddock and his sons, and at first I thought them wholly unfounded—so much so that I must confess to having thrown your original letter away in disgust.

But I came across an entry in the captain's journal that hinted at the animosity of which you wrote, and although I do believe that Captain Jeremiah meant well, his sons may have resented what he meant as kindness to your great-great grandfather.

Whatever occurred in the past, the fact remains that you are indeed a rightful member of the Braddock family, and as such, know that you are always welcome at the Harborside. I invite you to come and get to know your long-estranged family.

With utmost sincerity,
Irene Braddock"

The three sat in stunned silence, the clock seeming to tick louder than ever. Captain Braddock's face wrinkled into a frown as he voiced the question Katherine had been wanting to ask.

"Allegations? What allegations?"

Serena shook her head. "I don't know...Granny Braddock

never mentioned anything like that to me." She sighed. "I wish I could ask her."

"She mentioned the captain's journal. Do you know where that is?"

Captain Braddock and Serena looked at each other. "I've never come across it. Have you?" the captain asked.

"No. And until tonight, I had no idea such a treasure existed."

Katherine's heart leapt. She couldn't help but grin as she said, "Well, now we have *two* things to search for!"

Captain Braddock chuckled. "You'd better hand Serena a stack of papers, then." He turned to Serena, "Mind you don't lose that letter—or its envelope."

* * * *

Katherine woke the next morning wondering if she would ever feel rested again. It had been a late night, since she and the Braddocks were determined to sort through the whole box of papers she brought. The stack of recipes had doubled, and they found some old newspaper clippings which they set aside for the Harborhaven Historical Society, but they still hadn't found anything about the trust.

Serena had told her that Mr. Welch called again, saying he would only give them till the end of the week to come up with what they needed. Then, the property would be officially put up for sale. Unless they found out where the trust was and how to access it before Friday, the building could be sold to someone else and there would be nothing they could do about it.

If only we could find that information. Katherine thought with a sigh. She dragged herself out of bed and curled up in the window seat with a blanket and her Bible. Opening to the book of Proverbs, she read,

"Trust in the Lord with all thine heart; and lean not unto thine own understanding."

Her heart squeezed with conviction. *Lord, I want so much for the Harborside to be restored, it feels hard to trust You. Help me to trust, help me to remember that You have a good plan, and help me to hold loosely to how I want this all to end.*

Closing her Bible, she hugged it to her chest and gazed out into the inky blue of the early morning. After a few minutes, she let out a deep sigh, bowed her head and prayed, *Thy will be done.*

* * * *

"What?" Dishes rattled as Katherine rolled the tea cart over the kitchen threshold. "You mean there's some sort of long-lost relative somewhere, and their Gran never told them?"

"That's right." Katherine helped Sally wheel the cart to the first table and started setting out plates and silverware.

"But why did he never come visit like she said for him to?"

"He never opened the letter." Katherine glanced over at Sally, noticing that she now laid the silverware down with a quick, decided precision. *I wonder when that happened?* She suddenly felt she had missed something important in all the hectic struggle of the past week.

"Oh." Sally shrugged then looked up to meet Katherine's

gaze with inquisitive eyes. "Well, what are they going to do about it?"

"Do?"

"Yes, I mean, are they going to write again? Or track down this long-lost relative somehow?"

Katherine frowned. "I don't know. We were all just so excited at the thought of Captain Jeremiah's journal, we didn't talk about much else for a while."

"But don't you think they will want to meet this man?"

"I'm sure they will." The old fear began quietly tugging at Katherine's heart. Taking a stack of plates off the cart, she moved to a different table and began setting them out, trying to silence the nagging whispers of "*What if?*"

* * **

Katherine was well-ensconced in what the captain called "the land of arithmetic" balancing the ledger later that afternoon when the shop bell and a blast of cold air made her look up.

"What are you doing here?" Beaming, she jumped up and went to meet her visitors as Serena wheeled the captain in a wheelchair through the front door.

"He had an appointment today, and since we were already out of the house, we decided to stop by for a bit and say hello."

Captain Braddock raised his bushy eyebrows. "Oh, is *that* the way it happened?"

Serena laughed. "I was trying to be generous, Jeremiah,

and not let on how grumpy you got at the idea of going straight home."

Katherine chuckled and moved the old armchair to the other side of the wood stove. "Well, however it happened, I'm glad you came! Let's park the captain over here where it's warm, and I'll put the kettle on. It's chilly out there, and besides, I have a surprise for you."

Katherine breezed off to the kitchen, more butterflies in her stomach than she had felt for years. She put the kettle on, took down the teapot and reached for a shipping box on the counter. As she opened it, she breathed in deeply. The scent of cinnamon, chicory, and a spice she couldn't place filled the closet-like room as she opened the pouch of tea. *Yes. It's time.*

She had been wondering how to broach her new idea with the captain, and this seemed like just the right opportunity. Although both Braddocks had a strong family loyalty that led them to be reluctant to change anything about the Harbor-side, Serena had a sense of the practical and could usually help her brother see past his initial resistance to the thought of making even small changes to the Harborside.

While she waited for the water to boil, she rejoined the Braddocks in the shopfront. Picking up Tommy's stool from where it usually stood tucked into a corner, Katherine set it at the captain's feet. Carefully lifting his injured leg onto the stool, she noticed the sturdy boot-like cast. "This is new, isn't it?"

"Yes. And the doctor says I can put weight on my ankle, but it hurts more than I like to admit whenever I do." He grimaced, then put on his old expression of mock-sternness. "But don't you go tellin' her that." He nodded toward Serena who stood near the shelves with a dust rag in hand. She wasn't dusting though. She was standing completely still.

Katherine crossed the room and put a hand on Serena's arm. "You knew about the *Anne*, right?"

"Yes." Serena said softly, her voice catching. "But it didn't seem real until now. Such a treasure..."

"I know," Katherine whispered, not trusting her own voice.

Serena gave her a long look, then a little smile. "I believe you do know."

Just then, the tea kettle began singing and Katherine rushed off to make the tea.

In the kitchen, she swirled the hot water around the pot to warm it, just like the captain had taught her. Then she dumped the water into the sink and spooned in the loose tea. When she poured hot water over it, the steam engulfed her in a cloud of spices and orange peel. She smiled. Surely they wouldn't be able to resist.

Katherine set three cups on the mahogany tea tray with its inlaid starburst and handles worn smooth by generations of Harborside hands. As she set the teapot next to the cups, she glanced up at a shelf and, on an impulse, added the honey-pot as well.

"My, that's an interesting-smelling brew you've got there, Katherine. What is it?" Captain Braddock shifted in his seat as Katherine set an old tilt-top tea table next to him.

"You'll see." she set the tea tray on the table with a playful wink, while trying to calm the nervous jitters in her stomach.

"I think it smells heavenly," Serena said, sinking gracefully into the chair on the other side of the wood stove. "And tea by the stove on a winter's day—it's the good old days come back again, Jeremiah." She looked across at her brother with an expression Katherine recognized. It was the look of memory.

"It is indeed." Captain Braddock met his sister's gaze with unusual softness.

Katherine quietly poured out the tea, setting the tea strainer carefully out of sight behind the teapot. She wanted them to taste the tea before forming an opinion about the ingredients.

Handing the cups around, she smiled, trying to seem calm and collected. "It's good you both came in today, because I've been wanting your opinion on this."

"What is it?" the captain repeated.

"Opinion first, then details." Katherine moved the table over and placed a folding chair next to the captain, forming a sort of circle around the wood stove.

She watched as they sipped, amused, in spite of her anxiousness, at the similarity of their expressions.

"Well?" the question burst out of her before she could stop it.

Captain Braddock set the cup down in his saucer and stared at the reddish-brown liquid. He took another sip. "Cinnamon. Cardamom. Orange peel..." his voice trailed as he stared down again, pondering the substance before him.

"Chicory." Serena added, taking another sip. "and, is that...chamomile?"

"Yes." Katherine rubbed her palms together. "And apples"

"And...Allspice, I think?" Serena smiled. "What a lovely combination it all makes!"

Katherine tried to mask her sigh of relief. "You like it?"

"Yes. I do. What about you, Jeremiah, what do you think of it?"

Captain Braddock's face remained somber. "It's an herbal infusion, is that right?"

Katherine nodded. "It's from Israel. I stumbled across it while researching a Persian tea a customer mentioned. I never did find the Persian blend, but this sounded so interesting, I took a chance and ordered some." She held her breath, waiting for his reaction.

"We haven't sold herbal teas at the Harborside before." His expression changed to one Katherine could only describe as dubious.

"But that's not *exactly* true, Jeremiah." Serena interjected gently, taking another sip. "Granny told me once that Lizzy used to make her own blends of herbal infusions to sell in the shop. In fact, she had a little tea garden growing in that enclosed part of our yard. That's why it's so wild in there, all those herbs gone to seed—literally."

Katherine felt her eyes widen. "Really?"

"Yes." Serena studied her for a moment. "I'll show you next time you're over in the daylight."

Something like a door opened inside Katherine, and she felt a sudden certainty of direction, a widening of the idea she had been toying with. "I'd love that!"

"But back to this tea," Captain Braddock said, with such sternness that Katherine almost missed the quick twinkle in his eye. "It's good. We'll stock it."

Katherine nearly upset the tea table as she jumped up. "Then you'll have to try it with honey."

19

Treasure Hunt

"What are you doing with all that paper?" Tommy looked up at Katherine as she brought another stack of papers down from Granny's sea chest in the secret room.

"It's a sort of treasure hunt."

Tommy's eyes lit up. "Really? Can I help?"

"Maybe... but it's not pirate treasure or anything exciting like that. I'm looking for a very important paper." She chuckled at his obvious disappointment. "Sorry to get you all excited, but the paper really is a treasure." She settled into the chair by the fire, while Tommy took his favorite seat on the little stool nearby.

"What kind of treasure's made out of paper?" Tommy peered skeptically into the box of papers in Katherine's lap.

"Well," Katherine began, setting the box down on the floor and pulling out an untidy sheaf of papers. "You know how the

Harborside is like one little wooden building inside this big long brick building?"

"Yeah."

"The Harborside used to be the whole big building, but many years ago it was sold."

Tommy nodded sagely. "Cap'n told me."

"The Braddocks have been saving money all these years, just to buy back the rest of the building, but we don't know where the money is."

"So we're looking for a map?" Tommy's eyes lit up again.

"I suppose you could say it's a sort of a map. But it will probably look like a boring old bank paper."

"Oh." Tommy seemed to be considering. "Can I help?"

Katherine thought for a moment. "Yes, I think you can. I'll look at the papers, and you can put what I find into piles on the captain's desk."

"Yay!" he gave a little hop. "I hope we find the treasure map!"

"Me too." Katherine picked up a stack of papers and prayed silently, *Lord, help us find it!*

* * * *

By the time Tommy's mother came to pick him up that evening, all they had found were the usual receipts, recipes, and newspaper clippings, along with a few invoices which Katherine tucked away to compare with their current tea suppliers.

Wearily, she turned the lock on the shop door, pulled

down the window shade, and mounted the spiral staircase once again.

The lamps below in the shopfront gave just enough light for Katherine to see by as she went to the sea chest and raised the lid. She paid little attention to the stack she took out and placed on the floor, easing the lid gently closed with a sigh for how much was still left inside.

Picking up the papers, she headed back down the spiral staircase and plopped the stack into a box. As she did so, the papers slid to one side, exposing a manilla envelope with *First Bank of Harborhaven* and a logo stamped on one corner.

Barely able to breathe, Katherine pulled the envelope out, and with trembling fingers, slid the contents out enough to catch the words "put in trust."

With a squeal, she hugged the envelope to her, then rushed around, spreading out the already dying coals in the wood stove, turning off lights, and flinging her scarf, jacket and hat on as fast as she could. Tucking the envelope safely into her bag, she took one last look around the shop before locking up and walking hurriedly down the street.

The wind buffeted her as she walked, but she hardly noticed. *This might be it!* She thought over and over. *Thank you, Lord!*

* * * *

Katherine stopped by Miss Harriet's only long enough to get the keys to Mrs. James' car and let Sally know what was going on. The two had squealed and clutched each other's hands, jumping up and down like a couple of schoolgirls.

Katherine chuckled as she pulled up outside the Braddock house. *So mature.* But she knew she and Serena would probably repeat the performance, only without so much jumping.

Running up the steps to the door, Katherine knocked rapidly. Serena opened the door looking concerned, but one look at Katherine's face told her the news.

"You found it?" Serena's eyes were wide, and she looked as if she were afraid to hope.

"I think so." Katherine said, feeling another jump and squeal fit coming on, but containing herself with effort.

"You'd better come in, then."

* * * *

Katherine sat on the floor by the crackling fire, feet curled up under her wool skirt. The captain sat in his favorite chair, and Serena on an old sofa nearby. Katherine wondered if the captain was as nervous and excited as she felt. She glanced over at him and saw that he was watching Serena's face closely.

Minutes passed, and the clock ticked. No one moved while Serena read through the contents of the envelope. Finally, she looked up. A grin spread across her face. "Well, it's all here. The trust does exist. The money is held at the bank here in Harborhaven, and the trustee is the bank manager."

"Mr. Patten?" Katherine's surprise faded into a frown. "How come he didn't ever tell you?"

"He couldn't. From what this says, I gather the bank is only supposed to communicate directly with the designated beneficiary, which according to this, is me, and only upon request. And I never knew to ask him about it."

"And how much is there?" Captain Braddock's tone was even, his face thoughtful.

"I don't know. This only states how much she added to it when she made me the beneficiary... which isn't much." She scanned the papers again, then set them down next to her. "I guess I'll just have to make a visit to the bank tomorrow."

* * * *

Sally was wiping down the kitchen counters as Katherine came in.

"I'm so sorry I left you to do everything by yourself. You must be exhausted."

"No more than usual," Sally smiled. "As Auntie H. said when I signed on, this place isn't exactly a one-woman operation."

"And don't I know it. But we aren't meant to *have* to handle it alone anymore, and I'm sorry it ended up this way."

"It couldn't be helped. Besides, I'm getting experience. There are so many little jobs I didn't notice before because Auntie H. always just quietly did them."

"You'll be an expert in every bit of it by the time she comes back." Katherine chuckled, remembering how she had struggled through the same thing herself. "But tell me honestly, how is it going?"

Sally thought for a moment before replying. "At first, I couldn't tell," she tossed the rag into the laundry crate by the back door. "I mean, I was just trying to hang on, trying to keep people's orders coming and remember to bring their checks. But this week, I've felt like I'm getting the hang of it. Like my head's finally above water and I can breathe."

Katherine nodded, "I know what you mean. I've started to get to that point over at the Harborside now."

"Still..." Sally threw Katherine a grin. "I'll be happy to have Auntie H. back and everything normal again."

"Me too," said Katherine, with an inward uneasiness that questioned if "normal" would ever actually return.

* * * *

"What about the Harborside?" Captain Braddock asked, brows drawn and mouth crinkled in disapproval.

"I left a sign that said '*Closed for Lunch.*' I used my very nicest cursive writing and placed it prominently on the door."

He still looked unconvinced, so Katherine tried again.

"Besides, when was the last time you had a customer at this time of day?"

Captain Braddock's frown deepened, and he opened his mouth to speak, then slowly melted into a chagrined chuckle. "I suppose I can't argue with you there." He threw out his arms. "Welcome to the library."

Katherine happily gazed around her. This was a room she had never been in before. It had tall French doors that led out onto a tangle of plants and a tall mass of ivy. The walls were lined with bookshelves, and these were filled with old, leather or clothbound books, many in the ornate style so particular to Victorian times. Walking over to one of the shelves, she ran a finger lightly over the spines, reading the titles.

"*Homer's Odyssey...The Count of Monte Cristo... Moby Dick... A Sailor's Guide to Wind and Wave...*" Pulling out a thick volume, she chuckled.

"What is it?" Captain Braddock asked.

"*The Ashley Book of Knots*. This looks like a good book for Tommy." She handed it to the captain and chuckled again. "He's forever asking me to tie his shoes. A basic understanding of knots would be good for him."

"That's so. I've tried to teach him to tie his shoes, but it just doesn't stick, somehow. Needs to, though. Maybe a book of knots and a length of sail rope to practice on would help."

Katherine smiled. "It's worth a try."

The two talked and laughed as they waited for Serena to return from her meeting with Mr. Patten. The captain was almost back to his old self, and Katherine relished the chance to just sit and chat like they used to.

After a while Captain Braddock leaned forward. "What is it yer tryin' not to ask me, Missy?"

Katherine's eyes widened in surprise. "How—"

"I know yer look. You've got something on yer mind, but you don't think you should ask it."

Katherine shook her head in astonishment. "It's that obvious?"

He chuckled. "Only to me, Missy. Only to me." He shifted his leg to a more comfortable angle on the footrest in front of him. "Now, then. Unfurl that troubled heart of yers."

"Well..." Katherine twisted the fringe of her scarf around one finger, searching for the words. "If there's enough money in the trust to buy the rest of the Harborside block..."

"Yes?"

"What do you plan to do with it?"

Captain Braddock leaned forward. "I think the question of the hour is, what do *you* plan to do with it? I know you must have yer ideas, otherwise you wouldn't have been so excited about it, nor worked quite so hard to find the paperwork about the trust."

Katherine looked down, suddenly shy. "I do have some ideas..."

"And what are they? Don't be afraid, my girl."

She looked up into his eyes, which shone with more gentleness than she remembered ever having seen there. Emboldened, she blurted, "What about a museum?"

He nodded soberly. "Tell me more."

"Well, the warehouse has so many separate entrances, we could set up whatever space we don't need for the shop with some of the Braddock's treasures, and maybe have some signs printed, or do some sort of tour, explaining the history of the Harborside and sharing all the wonderful stories you've shared with Tommy and me. That way, the visitors would get a taste of the Harborside's legacy to go with their tea."

The captain thought a few minutes, then looked up, beaming. "Yer heart's with the Harborside, and yer mind's a sharp one, with a practical bent to it." He nodded. "Start plannin' yer museum, Missy."

He paused, then reached out to squeeze her hand as he added, "I trust you."

20

Harborside United

"Well?" Katherine and Captain Braddock both asked at once as Serena appeared in the doorway.

She stood for a moment on the threshold, her face drawn into a dramatically tragic frown, then grinned and clapped her hands. "We have enough—*more* than enough!"

Katherine felt tears well up in her eyes. She lifted her heart in silent gratitude to God as Serena and the captain talked over the details.

"It's ours as-is, but Mr. Patten said whatever money is left over would be fine to use for upkeep and repairs of the building." Serena sank into a chair, looking bright, cheerful, and exhausted all at once. "Oh, and Mr. Welch is selling it with, as he put it 'all the junk inside.' I suppose we'll find out what that means. I do hope it hasn't been used as someone's garbage dump." She hugged a needlepoint pillow and beamed at them. "Still... it's *ours* again."

"The Harborside will be whole." Captain Braddock said, eyes shining.

Katherine's throat tightened with emotion. She smiled at her friends, her heart silently shouting what her voice couldn't speak: *Thank You, Lord!*

* * * *

"You mean they've really got it?" Sally almost shouted the words.

Katherine turned the water on to fill the sink. "Yes. The sale closes in three months, since they have to go through the trust and all. But the contract has been signed, and it's as good as theirs!"

"I just can't believe it."

"I know, and there's more. The captain and Serena both agreed to let me start planning for a Harborside museum with some of the new space!"

Sally squealed and hugged Katherine, then, pulling a serious face, picked up a dish rag and flung it at her friend. "Now, then. These dishes aren't going to clean themselves. You wash, I'll dry."

Katherine laughed and swished her rag through the water to dissolve the dish soap. Soon the sink was filled with suds and Katherine began the comfortingly familiar chore.

As Sally rubbed the first teacup with her towel, she asked, "Did you ever find out what they're going to do about the letter?"

Katherine looked down at the suds she was rinsing off a saucer. "No. I didn't." Raising her head, she met Sally's concerned gaze. "I've thought about it, and worried about it more than I like to admit... but I've decided that's something I need to leave with God."

Sally nodded, her face sober. "I've something of the same kind myself."

"Really?" Katherine rinsed another cup and handed it to her friend. "Can you tell me?"

"It's my Dad. I haven't seen him since... well, you know I ran off pretty quick after my brother died, and never looked back. But now... I started to feel like I needed to write to him, to clear the air, at least about my running away. I know it must have hurt him dreadfully, especially right after losing my brother."

Katherine nodded. "That sounds like a good thing to do."

"Well, I talked with Auntie H. and eventually, I decided to. But then we went off for the New Year and I didn't get around to mailing my letter until the day after I got back here."

"And have you heard anything in reply?"

"That's the thing I have to leave with God, as you said. I never did hear, and I might not ever hear. For all I know, he may never read it." She looked down at the plate in her hands and moved her towel in methodical circles. "I may try again eventually, but for now, I feel I've done what was right, and need to just leave it alone."

Katherine dried her hands and put an arm around her friend. "I understand," she said softly. "And I'll be praying."

Sally returned her hug. "Thanks, Katherine."

* * * *

"Welcome home!" Katherine flung her arms around Mrs. James as she came through the doorway.

"Oh, Dearie. I'm glad to be here." Mrs. James wrapped Katherine in a motherly embrace before holding her at arm's length and eyeing her closely. "Now, how are you? Tell me truly."

"I'm fine. Really. It's been like a roller coaster, but it seems like the scary bit is over with and now—oh, I have so much to tell you!"

"And how is the Captain?"

"He's improving little by little. Serena's still here, by the way, and wants you to visit."

"Oh, that's all very good news!"

"But you haven't heard the rest of it."

"The rest?"

"*Auntie!*" Sally ran out from the kitchen and into Mrs. James' outstretched arms. "We've missed you ever so much!"

"And I've missed you—both of you!" Releasing Sally, she looked from one to the other. "Now, any chance of some tea while we get caught up?"

"I'll go." Sally offered, beaming at her aunt. "You two just sit and relax."

"Thank you, Sally. Katherine, let's sit by the window, and you can tell me all about the rest of the good news."

Katherine filled Mrs. James in on everything at the Harborside while Sally went off to make tea. After a while, the singing of the kettle brought up a new subject.

"How did Sally do?" Mrs. James said quietly.

"I haven't been around much to watch how she was with the customers, but as far as I can tell, they seem pleased with her, and I've noticed a new sort of...something. Confidence, maybe. I don't think she's dropped anything in a week, and she's standing taller and expressing herself better. She deserves a good day or two off, though, for all the hard work and extra hours she's put in while I was at the Harborside."

"Well, from all you say, it sounds like it was a difficult time, but God brought you both safely through it, and with good deal of growing to show for it." Mrs. James smiled sympathetically.

Just then, Sally appeared, carrying the tea.

"I see what you mean, Katherine," Mrs. James appraised her niece with delight. "Sally, I can tell already that you've done a good job while I was away, just by the way you carried that tray."

"What? Just by that?" Sally raised her eyebrows and blushed in pleased embarrassment.

"Yes. You used to carry the trays tentatively, with your shoulders rounded forward like this—" she hunched herself forward to demonstrate. "But now you're standing tall and the tray is neither shaking nor being dropped. You look exactly like you know what you're doing."

She stood and put her arms around her niece. "And what's more, you have the air of one who's discovered *why* she's doing it."

"Tell her about Rosie." Katherine prompted as Sally sat with them.

"Oh, yeah. Well, she'd been acting different... sad, I suppose. Anyway, I've been looking for ways to be extra kind to her, and Katherine told me what kind of tea to give her."

Mrs. James reached across the table and squeezed Sally's hand. "I'm sure that took a good deal of humility to reach out."

"I didn't even get a chance to tell Katherine yet, but yesterday, Rosie stayed a bit longer, and ended up the only customer for a while. I brought her another cup of tea and made one for myself, and sorta plunked myself down at her table."

"You did?" Katherine leaned forward, shocked at her friend's boldness.

"I told her I could tell she's been sad about something, and asked what it was." Sally paused and took a sip of her tea.

"And did she tell you, Dearie?" Mrs. James asked gently.

"Yes. Trouble with her kids. Turns out it was just as you said. She just wants to be loved. Anyway I ...well, I told her that I'd be praying for her—and I have been."

Katherine and Mrs. James exchanged happy smiles across the table.

"I suppose that means we won't have any more dramatic incidents in the tearoom." Mrs. James chuckled. "I have to say I'm glad about that. And I'm so pleased to see how you both have grown during this difficult few weeks."

She reached out and took their hands in hers. "It's a joy to come back and find you both still seeking out those 'old paths' and finding rest for your souls through all this turmoil. And now that I'm home again, I hope you can both take time to find rest for your bodies as well."

* * * *

The next day, Katherine woke to the familiar sound of Mrs. James starting the morning baking. She nestled her head into her pillow as she listened, wondering how two people performing the same tasks the same way could sound so different from each other. Then, with a smile, she rolled onto her side and drifted back asleep.

* * * *

When Katherine woke again, she fully enjoyed the luxury of a slow morning. The Harborside didn't open till ten that day, and, although eager to start planning for the museum, she took her time getting up and ready, spending extra time curled up in the window seat with her Bible.

When she finished reading her usual few chapters, she flipped back to the book of Jeremiah and found the verse that had become precious, not just for its promise, but for its reality in her life.

"Thus saith the Lord, Stand ye in the ways, and see, and ask for the old paths, wherein is the good way, and walk therein, and ye shall find rest for your souls."

The words were so familiar by now, she could have recited them with her eyes closed. But as she read a new gratitude filled her heart, as she noticed how the verse ended.

"But they said, We will not walk therein."

She suddenly realized how close she had come to missing out on the soul-deep rest she had found in God. At so many moments of decision, she could have chosen to go her own way, to do her own thing instead of letting God guide her—and everything would have been different.

Without God, she would still be dully moving through life, overwhelmed by the pain in her heart and the darkness of her past. As she sat and watched the blanket of clouds over the harbor slowly change from midnight blue to the pale grey of morning, her heart once again overflowed in what had become her favorite prayer: *Thank You, Lord!*

21

Dilemma and Decision

"Katherine, do you have a few minutes?" Mrs. James asked as Katherine came down the stairs, buttoning her jacket.

"Yes, I think so, although I need to get to the Harborside." She tried to keep her tone light, crossing the room with quick strides, to mask the uneasiness that suddenly gripped her.

"It can open late today," another voice said from behind her.

"Serena! What are you doing here?" Katherine was pleased to see her friend, but it did seem strange for her to be at the tea shop before it opened.

"We've been having a chat, Dearie. Come and sit down." Mrs. James motioned Katherine into a chair at Serena's table before taking another herself.

Katherine looked from one lady to the other, not sure what was coming next. The verse flitted through her mind:

Perfect love casteth out fear. Katherine felt a wave of peace wash over her. *I trust You,* she prayed silently, meaning it.

The two women looked at each other, as if deciding how to begin. Serena spoke first.

"I have watched you these last few weeks, and seen how you have invested in the Harborside. It isn't just a job to you, is it?"

Katherine shook her head. "I..." she blushed and looked down for a moment. Then she met Serena's eyes. "the Harborside feels like home to me."

Serena nodded. "I know. I could tell that first day I met you, when you came down from the secret room and thought I was a customer. Remember?"

Katherine chuckled at the memory. "I had no idea it was you."

Serena took a sip of her tea before going on. "Well, I know you and Jeremiah have talked about what to do with this new space we will have, and I think your idea of a museum is wonderful! It will take time to set up and manage, though.—more time than we have you contracted for."

Katherine's stomach tightened a little. "Yes...I suppose so."

"So that's why Jeremiah and I would like to offer you a full-time position at the Harborside."

Katherine tried to speak, but couldn't form the words. Her heart beat away happily, leaving her a little breathless. But then she looked at Mrs. James and realized what a full-time position would mean. "But.." she forced out, her voice barely above a whisper, "Miss Harriet's..."

The other lady smiled gently. "Sally did so well in my

absence, and I don't have any lengthy trips coming up. I think we can manage here if you want to take this position."

"Jeremiah is nearly well enough to help with some of the administrative details now, though you might keep an eye on his ledger work for the next few weeks." Serena winked, then her face sobered. "But, to be honest, I don't like the idea of him there alone all the time, especially until his leg is fully healed. It would be a help, not just to the Harborside, but to me as well if you would be willing to be full time."

Katherine felt like her heart was playing tug-of-war with itself. She loved working at Miss Harriet's and she loved Sally and Mrs. James, who had both become so dear to her. But the Harborside was home and the captain—she knew he would need more help than ever now. And she *wanted* to be the one to help. *What should I do?* She prayed silently.

"Think about it for a day or so, and let me know." Serena said gently. Katherine looked at the women again. Both were beaming, confident that this was the right thing for her.

"I'll let you know when I'm sure." She said, not certain how she would ever decide.

* * * *

The day moved past in a blurry fog. Katherine decided dusting jars was about all she was fit to handle for the day, and her inattention nearly cost her the loss of yet another antique tea bowl. It had slipped out of her hand as she wiped it with the rag, her mind on the relentless tug-of-war inside her. Thankfully, she had caught the bowl in time. She shuddered, remembering how close she had come to breaking it.

Unlocking the door, she threw her keys onto the table and crossed to the window seat. Curling her legs under her, she grabbed a pillow and hugged it tightly to her. *What should I do?* she thought, leaning her head wearily against the cool glass of the windowpane. *Lord, help me decide.*

If she took the position at the Harborside, she would be thrust into something of a new life. No more bussing tables, taking orders, and prepping food. No more morning baking or dishes in the evening.

Part of her felt ready for a change, but she was used to how things were. Was she willing to give up Miss Harriet's and work only for the Harborside? *Am I willing to do it if God wants me to?* The question softly filled her mind, while conviction pressed at her heart.

She tossed the pillow aside and knelt next to the window seat. *Lord, I trust You. I want Your will, no matter what. Please, guide me.* Her heart yearned for everything to just stay the same, but was that really the right decision? She stayed on her knees, determined to pray until God showed her what to do.

* * * *

Clear morning light peeped over the rooftops as Katherine drifted awake. Gradually, she realized she had fallen asleep praying. She eased herself up onto the window seat and slowly moved her legs to work the stiffness out. Gazing out the window, she noticed that the clouds had gone from her heart and mind, as well as from the sky. She no longer felt torn. She knew the answer she would give Serena.

* * * *

When she arrived at the Harborside, the captain and Tommy were already there.

"Good mornin' Katherine!" Captain Braddock gave her a happy grin she hadn't seen in a while.

"Good morning. It's good to see you two here." Looking over at Tommy, she asked, "But what about school? You aren't skipping just to hang out with the captain, are you?" She put on her sternest frown and shook her finger at the boy.

He laughed. "Nope. There was no school today, so I came here instead."

"And I am very glad you did, my boy. It's been too long since I saw you."

Tommy's face shone with delight. "Any more rags, Katherine? I asked Cap'n, but he said to ask you."

"Yes, I washed them, but haven't put them away yet. I'll get some for you." She went into the kitchen to grab the stack of clean rags she had folded the day before.

As she returned to the shopfront, Tommy was sitting at the captain's feet, listening to the story of the *Anne's* first voyage, mouth open, eyes wide, enthralled by the captain's description of the pirate raid. *Just as though he'd never heard it before.* Katherine smiled and leaned her head against the doorway. After a few minutes, she shifted slightly and her foot met a creaky floorboard.

The distinct sound caught the captain's attention and he turned. With a questioning look he asked, "What're you thinking of, my girl?"

With a smile on her face and joy in her heart, she said simply, "Home."

The captain's eyes lit with realization. "You've decided, then?"

"Yes. I'll be working full time at the Harborside now." Peace flooded Katherine's heart as she said the words.

"Does that make you the Harborside's girl, like I'm the Harborside's boy?" asked Tommy.

Flinging a rag into the boy's lap, she mussed his hair and said, "I think you must be right."

"Katherine of the Harborside... has a ring to it, don't you think?" Captain Braddock winked. "Now, how about those jars that need dusting?"

* * * *

As she turned the heavy key in the Harborside's antique lock, Katherine took in a deep breath and smiled. The sun had just set, and the sky still clung to its shades of pink and orange, though the gathering dusk was quickly replacing them with purple and blue.

She walked around to the back of the building and headed homewards along the wharf, running her fingers along the red Victorian brick of the Harborside, its surface rough and solid to her touch.

She stopped when she reached the new section of the warehouse and laid her hand on the wall, trying to imagine what might be inside. Closing her eyes, she pictured a large space, perhaps with shelves along the walls, filled to the brim with artifacts that told the story of the Harborside and the Braddock family.

Opening her eyes, Katherine continued on her way. She had peace, direction, and all the freshness of a new vision for the future. She had never been happier.

After all the uncertainty of the past few months, she rested in this new certainty that she was where she belonged, where God *meant* her to belong. She was ready for the next chapter.

Learning Ladyhood Press

For more books by this author

Devotional Commentaries

Wholesome Fiction

The Hymns for the Heart Devotional series

Visit Learning Ladyhood.com